# THE
# SAINT BERNARD MEMOIRS

## JENNY KANE

First published in 2025 by Creative Horse Studio

Creative Horse Studio
Guilford, Indiana

ISBN 979-8-9939468-1-8 (hardcover)

ISBN 979-8-9939468-0-1 (paperback)

Printed and bound in United States of America
10 9 8 7 6 5 4 3 2 1

Cover artwork by Sarah Brantley

Design & typesetting by Creative Horse Studio

**Dedicated to Norman and Stanley,**
the first Saint Bernards to capture my heart.
Thank you for inspiring a lifelong love.

These pure, simple things help to light up my smile,
Sparking bliss as I gaze at my Saint Bernard pile.
Open windows inviting a cool, gentle breeze,
A heartfelt "God bless you" whenever I sneeze.
A candle's aroma, a warm cozy fire,
My twenty-year soulmate, ablaze with desire.
Endorphins ignite as I run fast and free,
My daughters' embrace, and their time spent with me.
A savory meal topped with good conversation;
Shared with family and friends make the perfect equation.
Thank you kindly, Dear Lord, for this beautiful day.
Help me use all my gifts to show others the way.

# The Saint Bernard Memoirs

In 1994, at the age of twelve years old, I had finished a babysitting job and was bidding my farewells to the family for whom I had worked. While saying goodbye, a friend of theirs pulled in with two magnificent creatures riding in the back of a pickup truck—obviously not a safe form of transportation, but the least of my concerns at the time. Their size was such that they took up the entire bed of the truck. They had streams of drool dangling from their jowls, a coat of dense fur that covered my entire being, and the most soulful and human eyes that I had ever seen in an animal.

They were exquisite; I was mesmerized. From that moment, I was smitten with a fondness for the breed that would remain with me into adulthood. The movies *Cujo* and *Beethoven* featured Saint Bernard dogs, but encountering one in real life filled me with youthful joy and awe. I silently vowed that one day, I would have a Saint Bernard of my own. From then on, whenever someone asked me, "What do you want to do when you grow up?" I would respond, "Live on a farm and have seven Saint Bernards."

I had begged my parents for a dog for years—specifically a Saint Bernard. My family of six lived in a two-bedroom, one-bathroom Cape Cod, so I knew that my vision of owning a Saint Bernard was out of the question and would have to wait. I've always said that the best part of being an adult is that if you want a puppy, you go out and get yourself a puppy!

After years of asking, when I reached the age of thirteen, my persistence finally paid off. Few childhood moments compare to the joy of getting your first puppy—it's a memory eternally etched into my mind. I was allowed to adopt a small abandoned mutt whom I named Chance. He got the name from my almost daily question: "What are the *chances* of me getting a dog?" Chance brought much joy and quality to my life, and he lived to the ripe old age of seventeen.

For as long as I can remember, I've had three key desires in life—to be a wife, a mother, and to own a Saint Bernard! On October 29, 1999, at the age of seventeen, I collected the mail and stumbled upon a horoscope that read, *Capricorn, you know the person you're with is not the one for you. You already have a secret admirer waiting in the wings, so make yourself available.* I had been routinely crossing paths with a striking young man in my daily travels. I instantly thought of him and felt butterflies in my stomach.

I quickly skimmed to *Gemini* because that was the zodiac sign of the inconsequential boyfriend that I had at the time. My eyes widened as I read, *Gemini, is your relationship telling you something you don't want to hear? You know in your heart that this person is not the one for you.* Taken by surprise, I sprinted out to my car and tucked the horoscope under my front seat.

That evening, as I headed out with my friends, I proclaimed, "If I run into that cute guy that I've been telling you about, I'm going to get his phone number!" We went to a local high school football game and then headed to Skyline Chili for a bite to eat. I was facing the door, enjoying a cheese coney, when my future husband, whose name I didn't yet know was Brian, walked in.

My heart pounded as I walked confidently over to his table and asked him for his phone number, which he scribbled down onto a napkin. Twenty-six years later, that napkin remains on display in our home. It goes without saying that Brian was also a dog lover—a nonnegotiable trait when it came to being marriage material.

Brian and I always had a clear vision for what we wanted our future to look like. We got married in 2002 when our first daughter, Carly, was eleven months old. Our second daughter, Heidi, was born in 2004. We bought a house together, outgrew it, and eventually built two more. Early on, I had told Brian about my passion for owning a Saint Bernard. One of the very first gifts that he gave me while we were dating was a pair of Saint Bernard slippers. I still have them in my closet and wear them around the house.

Interestingly, Brian and I discovered that both his mother and grandmother had owned Saint Bernards whom they adored while growing up. Their names were Thumper and Hauser. At one time, I was able to see a photo of them both, but somehow the photos have been misplaced and we've searched for them to no avail.

In 2011, our daughters, Carly and Heidi, were ten and seven years old. We had always encouraged their love of animals, and believed that pet ownership was the perfect way to instill kindness and responsibility. Over the years, we'd had mice, hamsters, and bunnies, but had now reached the point where we could afford to welcome a dog into our family. Our girls were also responsible enough to help with the many tasks that came with caring for one.

My childhood dream was about to come true! Or so I thought...

The pursuit of the perfect Saint Bernard puppy was officially underway! I had been reading extensively about the breed and knew that I wanted a rough-coat male. We found a "dry mouth" breeder online who lived less than two hours away in Miamisburg, Ohio. Even better—the breeder was expecting a litter ready to go by Christmas morning! We quickly submitted our deposit to secure "pick of the litter."

On Christmas Eve, Brian and I excitedly drove to retrieve our bundle of joy whom we named Otis. All of his littermates had gone to their new homes the previous week. Otis was just six weeks old when we brought him home. Given that this was our first canine acquisition as adults, we were unaware that removing a puppy from their mother before the age of eight weeks can be detrimental and is even illegal in many states. Puppies need to remain with their mother and littermates until at least eight weeks of age in order to learn proper socialization, bite inhibition, and for overall behavioral development.

In hindsight, in addition to Otis's age, there were several indicators which should have compelled us to walk away. In actuality, a "dry mouth" Saint Bernard does not exist. There are certainly Saint Bernards that are bred to be less jowly, but they all drool (A LOT), and if a breeder is telling you otherwise, it's misleading at best. If at all possible, meeting both the dam and the sire is beneficial, as it affords you the opportunity to observe their temperaments firsthand. We never met Otis's sire (father), nor were we given the opportunity.

Christmas morning was magical and everything Brian and I had envisioned. The girls were ecstatic about our new family member, and my heart was brimming with joy as I watched a childhood dream come to fruition. It felt empowering to give our children something for which I had always yearned.

The first ten months with Otis were everything I had hoped for. We took him to parks and ballgames, exposing him to lots of different people and places. He seemingly loved everyone, and wherever we took him people asked to have their photo taken with him. The girls and I especially enjoyed observing people's reactions to Otis riding shotgun in my convertible.

Around the time that Otis turned a year old and had reached 150 pounds, Brian texted me during my evening waitressing shift and said, *Otis is acting really strange. The girls have friends over, and he's frantically pacing, whining, and shaking uncontrollably.*

I was perplexed and replied, *Just put him in his crate until he calms down.*

It was a busy night at work, with the holiday season approaching. I didn't give much more thought to the situation until I called Brian on my drive home.

Otis had eventually calmed down, so Brian had let him out of his crate, and he retreated to his bed. However, to our dismay, later that night when Carly's friend walked past him, Otis awoke, crept behind her, and bit her on the back, breaking the skin. I was astonished but grateful that the friend's parents were very understanding and reassuring. They suggested that perhaps it was a one-off incident and that it wouldn't happen again.

The situation made me uneasy, and I became hypervigilant, watching for any further signs of aggression. A few weeks later, we were at the park when a special-needs child politely asked to pet Otis. In the past, Otis had loved attention—especially from children, but after giving my consent, the child suddenly began to scream for no apparent reason, whereupon Otis aggressively lunged at him.

Fortunately, I had Otis leashed, and I was able to pull him away before anything catastrophic happened. Again, I had misgivings, but I felt that Otis's behavior might have been justified by the child's outburst.

Several months passed without incident. Then one afternoon during a game of family wiffle ball, Otis, completely unprovoked, charged aggressively toward a fence behind which my four-year-old nephew was playing. It was becoming difficult for me to trust Otis, and I grew hesitant to allow my girls to have friends over. I was confused and disappointed because my vision had always been to have a Saint Bernard that could accompany us on family outings and whom I could proudly show off.

The final indicator that we had a serious problem on our hands occurred when I took Otis for a walk to my in-laws'. Otis was eighteen months old at this point. Carly and Heidi had already arrived and were playing with a friend while Brian helped their friend's father with an outdoor project. The girls and their friend eagerly greeted Otis, and to my relief he wagged his tail gleefully and appeared excited to see them. Heidi took his leash and happily romped around the yard with him.

Less than ten minutes after we had arrived, Heidi let go of Otis's leash for some reason. My heart sank the moment I saw his eyes glaze over. He bolted toward Carly and her friend, who were now walking over the hill. I sprinted after Otis and reached him just as he tackled Carly's friend, pinning him to the ground and biting him in the bicep. My heart pounded. I had so much adrenaline coursing through me that, even though Otis far outweighed me, I managed to grab him by the collar and pull him off the understandably terrified and crying child.

Otis looked dazed and confused, as though he couldn't comprehend what he had done wrong. My entire body was trembling. I was angry and horrified by what I had just witnessed. Fighting back tears, I called out to Brian that I was taking Otis home.

My childhood dream had become more like a nightmare. I was devastated. I immediately called our trusted veterinarian. After discussing Otis's behavior with him and inviting a reputable trainer into our home to assess the situation, I accepted the unfortunate fact that keeping Otis wasn't feasible. I bawled my eyes out for days.

Our pets are part of the family, and I'm deeply committed to giving them the best life possible. However, the happiness and well-being of my husband and children take precedence. I will never jeopardize the life we've built together for a dog. When your veterinarian looks you in the eye and says, "This dog could take one of your children's faces off," and a trainer tells you, "I can work with this dog for thousands of hours, but I can't guarantee it won't attack again," you're left with an excruciating decision.

I explained the situation on my Facebook page, requesting sound advice from anyone who might have it to offer. Everyone was familiar with Otis and had watched him grow from just a clumsy bundle of oversized paws. People were dismayed by what had transpired regarding our beloved pet. As expected, the opinions were mixed, which only added to my confusion. But in my heart, I knew we couldn't keep Otis.

Several people suggested surrendering him to a Saint Bernard rescue, but Otis was a loose cannon, and I couldn't justify putting another family in harm's way. After several weeks of sharing our story and being completely transparent about the situation, one of Brian's cousins reached out to say she had found a farm willing to give Otis a home. I made it very clear that Otis couldn't be around children. We paid to have him neutered to ensure that he would never be bred. At that point, he was still intact—giant breed dogs like Saint Bernards shouldn't be neutered before eighteen months of age to support proper bone and joint development.

For weeks, I was overwhelmed with anxiety and found myself in tears more often than not. Sleep was elusive, and even simple routines like going for a morning run felt impossible. I was relieved that we had found a resolution, but I felt deep regret that things hadn't gone as planned. I couldn't imagine my life without a Saint Bernard, and I wasn't ready to give up on my dream.

I remember speaking with our veterinarian, who kindly reassured me, "This is extremely atypical for the breed. If a Saint Bernard is what you truly want, then you should have one. The chances of this happening again are very slim."

Otis was adjusting well to his new home. The solution was bittersweet at best, because I wanted his home to be with us. I followed up weekly to see how he was settling in. Around this time, I noticed multiple swollen lymph nodes in my neck and chest. I went to the doctor, who presumed I was fighting an infection and started me on a course of antibiotics. When those failed to resolve the issue, I was prescribed a different medication, which also proved unsuccessful.

At that point, my doctor recommended having a lymph node surgically removed and biopsied to rule out lymphoma. To say I was terrified would be an understatement.

The surgery was scheduled for the following week. I vividly remember how overly friendly and complimentary the nurses seemed, and I couldn't help but think, *They're just being nice because they think I'm dying.* The surgery itself was routine, and Brian took me home to recover.

That evening, my cell phone lit up, displaying my physician's number. My heart leaped in my chest. I will never forget hearing, "This is Dr. Nurre. I know how worried you've been, and I wanted to share the results with you right away. It's completely benign." I felt like I had been born again!

Although the cause of my swollen lymph nodes was never determined, I'm fully convinced that the stress of handling the situation with Otis was to blame. It reminded me that tomorrow isn't promised, but that shouldn't dissuade us from chasing our dreams. Instead, it should inspire us to live in the moment and embrace every opportunity. I grabbed my phone and typed *Saint Bernard puppies* into the search bar.

Two weeks later, Brian and I were headed to Memphis, Tennessee, to pick up our new puppy—Wilbur! It was an eight-hour drive one way, but the breeder had agreed to meet us halfway. Three hours into the trip, the breeder called to say that her truck had broken down and we'd have to make the entire trek. Brian and I nervously carried on, hoping there would actually be a puppy waiting for us when we arrived—and there was! A filthy, smelly, parasite-ridden little guy, but precious all the same. I lifted him into my arms, kissed his sweet nose, and prepared for the long drive home.

Wilbur sat on my lap the entire ride, demanding that the air conditioning be on full blast. If I turned it down even one notch, he would whine incessantly.

Once we arrived home with Wilbur and cleaned him up, I remember thinking that he smelled exactly like my beloved childhood blanket. Housebreaking Wilbur was much easier than it had been with Otis because it was summertime and we spent most of our days outdoors. Being outside in the mild early morning air was far more bearable than braving the howling wind with chattering teeth. When bringing home a puppy, that's definitely something to keep in mind.

We immediately hired a trainer to work with Wilbur. It was clear early on that Wilbur had a much calmer temperament than Otis. He was extremely gentle with Carly and Heidi, whereas Otis had often been rough and domineering. Otis had always been more aloof, while Wilbur was affectionate and deeply engaged with us. He took part in all of our family activities, and he genuinely seemed to believe that he was one of us. He especially loved swimming and would corral us all to shore, beaming with pride, convinced that he was rescuing us.

As summer turned to autumn, Brian and I began planning a fall vacation. Wilbur had already reached 100 pounds, but in my heart, I couldn't imagine leaving him behind. Both Brian and I drove small sedans, and it seemed nearly impossible to make the twelve-hour drive to Florida with a Saint Bernard in tow, but I was determined to find a way.

*Wilbur, proudly certain he's the hero of the moment, rescuing Heidi.*

I suggested to Brian that we remove the front passenger seat from his BMW so Wilbur could have that space. I would sit in the back with the girls. Brian looked at me like I was crazy, but he also knew that I wasn't going to take no for an answer. The decision was made!

As we prepared for our trip, I found myself thinking about Otis and decided to check in on him. I was taken aback to learn that he and another dog had burst through an electric fence, pulled down a jogger, and broken both of the man's arms. Tragically, Otis was humanely euthanized. My heart was again broken.

Seeing how different Wilbur was, and knowing that Otis had been raised in the same loving environment, reassured me that something had been deeply, and perhaps neurologically, wrong with Otis. During one of our many conversations with the veterinarian, the term "idiopathic aggression" came up. It's a rare and severe behavioral disorder in dogs that causes sudden, intense, and unpredictable aggression without warning. Episodes can last several minutes, and during or after them, the dog may appear dazed or confused. Then, just as suddenly, they return to normal.

By the time we made it to Florida, all of us felt as though we'd been tarred and feathered, but it was worth it to have Wilbur with us. We had made many stops along the way and the "puparazzi" were out in full force. Everywhere we went, Wilbur was a celebrity, and he embraced every second of the love he received.

I remember driving through a Starbucks and the barista exclaiming, "Your dog is so cool! Drinks are on me!" I think the awe factor that Saint Bernards possess is one of the many reasons that I became infatuated with the breed. Everyone adores a puppy, but the novelty often wears off as it reaches maturity. A Saint Bernard's intelligence and majesty become more pronounced with age.

*Wilbur basking in all his glory on Amelia Island, with Carly (11) and Heidi (9).*

Our vacation was spectacular! We spent every moment at the beach soaking up the sunshine and searching for shark teeth together. (It was the start of our collection, which has grown to over 10,000 teeth today.) Brian and I will always cherish the memory of how devoted and protective Wilbur was of Carly and Heidi. Whenever they were in the ocean, he never left their side. He jumped every wave with them, and when they would go under he would bark incessantly, licking their faces repeatedly when they resurfaced.

As we walked down the beach, Wilbur made plenty of friends and sat on countless laps as beachgoers snapped photos. When our trip ended, we received an email from the condo association from which we had rented, stating that Wilbur had been the talk of the island and had brought much joy to all who had the pleasure of crossing paths with him.

*"You can usually tell that a man is good if he has a dog who loves him." —W. Bruce*

When we returned home, I realized that the Feast Day of Francis of Assisi (October 4th) was approaching. I began searching online for a pet blessing that we could attend with Wilbur. A Catholic Church just around the corner was hosting one, and it became a yearly tradition for our family. It brought me comfort and reassurance after our experience with Otis. One year, while attending the event, we appeared on the front page of the local newspaper.

Wilbur held a special place at the center of our family. He was Brian's fishing buddy, Carly's loyal training partner during her BMX (bicycle motocross) sprint workouts, Heidi's trusty sidekick for every baking adventure, and truly my dream come true. He was the glue that held our family together, and we formed an even deeper connection during our evening walks. We became known as "the tiny family who walked the giant dog."

As we walked, we would use the opportunity to not only visit the cows and the neighbors who had come to know and love Wilbur, but to also discuss our hopes, dreams, and future aspirations. On one of those walks, Carly and Heidi told us that they wished we lived on a large plot of land instead of in a subdivision. Brian and I took their words to heart, and the search for land began almost immediately.

Several weeks later, Brian discovered a nineteen-acre lot in Guilford, Indiana that was exactly what we were looking for. It had a creek that ran along the front of the property and a nice pond. There were lots of woods, and we could envision the spot on which we would build our dream home. Our only concern was a run-down single-wide trailer on the adjacent property. It was a bit of an eyesore, but we agreed that it wasn't reason enough to pass up putting an offer in on the land.

We reached out to the listing agent right away, but were disappointed to learn that a verbal agreement had already been made with a cash offer. Most people probably would've walked away at that point, but something about this land felt worth fighting for. I decided to check the county records to find out who owned the land, hoping I might persuade them to reconsider. After finding a last name, I decided that I would start cold-calling everyone with that name listed in the Yellow Pages.

By sheer luck, the first person I called turned out to be the seller's brother who willingly gave me his number. I called him immediately, and after a two-hour conversation during which we discovered mutual friends and plenty of common ground, we made an offer that was $5,000 higher than the original. In the end, I was able to convince him to sell the land to us instead. He was happy with his decision because the previous buyer had planned to use the property solely for hunting, whereas we planned to build our dream home—something he had once hoped to do himself but never had the opportunity to make happen.

Moments like this are a reminder that if something truly matters, you should give it everything you've got! Don't let fear hold you back—the worst anyone can do is say no. I'd much rather take the chance and know than spend my life wondering what might have been. If I hadn't been gutsy enough to walk over to that table at Skyline when I was seventeen, the entire trajectory of my life may have been completely different. Just like then, taking the chance changed everything.

In August of 2014, we closed on the plot of land, and put our home on the market with no set plan of how everything would unfold. The only thing I was certain of was now that we had land, I wanted another Saint Bernard.

When we initially listed our home for sale, the market was stagnant. The process was frustrating, and we had a lot of potential buyers who wasted our time. We ended up removing our listing and taking some time to enjoy the best of both worlds—living in a subdivision with a park, yet having land that we could hike and explore.

In March of 2016 we relisted our home, "For Sale by Owner." Within forty-eight hours, we received two offers at full asking price. After accepting an offer, I told Brian that I was relieved no one had noticed the giant blob of drool dangling from the ceiling during the showing.

Our main concern was the fact that we had just forty-five days to vacate our residence, and we didn't have the foggiest idea where we were going. Brian and I both knew that if we rented somewhere, it would take funds away from building our dream home.

Suddenly a possible solution occurred to me. I looked at Brian and said, "What if we could convince the owner of that single-wide to sell it to us along with the additional two acres? Then we'd be on our land and we could get rid of the trailer after it served its purpose."

Brian looked at me in surprise and replied, "You'd really be willing to do that?" The idea seemed to make perfect sense to me, and was only a temporary situation. The first house we had built took us roughly a year, and we didn't anticipate this one taking any longer.

The next day, I knocked on the door of the single-wide but no one answered. Through word of mouth, we learned that the owner was a man named "Opie" who rented the place out. The previous renter had just moved. I felt as though the stars were aligning in our favor.

We tracked down a phone number for Opie, and within the week we had decided on an agreeable purchase price. Opie gave us immediate access so that we could begin getting the place move-in ready.

Just two weeks before we had to vacate our home, a friend of mine whom I had met through Wilbur's trainer, reached out. She was a well-known Saint Bernard breeder and prominent in the dog show world. She knew that I had been putting some feelers out for another Saint Bernard puppy and she was confident that she had found "the one."

She messaged his photo to me, and I couldn't help but smile. He was ten weeks old and awaiting a family. I quickly got in touch with his breeder who was located in Virginia, and she agreed to meet us halfway the following weekend—just one week before we had to vacate our house!

For the next week, Brian, the girls, and I chatted about potential names. We unanimously decided that "Opie" was the perfect fit, based upon the name of the man who had sold us the single-wide.

Brian and I were off on another road trip! The majority of our conversation revolved around how crazy we were to be picking up a puppy a week before our moving date. We were both really excited and agreed that if we were going to add another puppy to our family, we'd prefer to do it while we were living in the single-wide. That way the puppy would likely be broken of his potentially destructive habits before we moved into our new house.

We also discussed what features we wanted in the home we were going to build. Brian had already made the decision that not only would he design our home, but he would also physically build it—all while working his full-time job as a Creative Director and Web Developer.

When we arrived at our meeting spot, Opie's breeder gently placed him in my arms. With tears in her eyes she asked, "Do you like him? Is he what you expected?"

I replied, "He's everything I ever dreamed of," and I meant it wholeheartedly and with every ounce of my being.

After arriving home with Opie, we quickly realized that the only thing better than having one Saint Bernard was having two! I hadn't begun packing for our move and was completely distracted by how cute Wilbur and Opie interacted with each other. They were inseparable from the start.

*The unforgettable moment Opie's breeder, Jennifer Hanger, placed him into my arms.*

On May 8, 2016, we moved into the trailer. Carly was fourteen years old, and Heidi was eleven. It rained for an entire week. I had always been meticulous about my house, but quickly realized that I was fighting a losing battle with two Saint Bernards in a 900-square-foot space.

The first night we spent in the trailer, I couldn't help but remember what the wife of Opie—the man we bought the trailer from—had said at the closing: that she had once tried to sleep there but couldn't because rats were fighting underneath it all night. I found myself thinking, *What did I sign up for?*

*Opie moseys through the fort the girls built out of creek rock.*

During our first week in the trailer, the water heater gave out, the central air failed, the washing machine stopped working, we found that only the outlets on one side of the trailer functioned, the roof leaked, and the oven was completely infested with mice. I also somehow managed to wash a mouse! There was a brief moment of panic when I went to switch the laundry and thought it might be

Carly's hamster—thankfully, it wasn't. Despite it all, we were on our land, surrounded by the people and animals we loved most—and it was only temporary.

Wilbur was already familiar with our land because, by this point, we had owned it for a year and a half. There were only three other residences on our road and Wilbur and Opie instantly came to be known and loved. According to our neighbors, "Dogs always loved it back in the holler," and we were finding that to ring true.

We discovered that there were 260 acres behind us, 130 acres adjacent, and another 50 acres across the road. We were given permission from the owners to explore it all!

We spent every spare moment outdoors searching for deer sheds, mushrooms, and arrowheads. We hiked in our creek and built forts in the woods. Wilbur and Opie especially loved swimming with us in our pond. Nothing excited Opie more than going for a ride in our pedal boat. He spent hours rooting around the pond. His ears would perk up with excitement whenever a frog would splash into the water. Carly and Heidi hosted many campouts, and Wilbur and Opie swam in their company, probably believing that they were one of the gang.

*Left: An endearing look from Wilbur as we hunt for morel mushrooms on our land.*
*Right: Wilbur sniffs a morel mushroom.*

*Carly and Heidi, making treasured memories with Wilbur and Opie in our pond over the years.*

Brian was finishing our house plans, and we were looking forward to breaking ground. We had come to the realization that it would be nearly impossible to break ground before spring. In light of the fact that we didn't have a mortgage, Brian and I decided to purchase an RV and spend our summer traveling to BMX Nationals in the hope of finding a racing sponsorship for Carly. We purchased a 1994 C-Class RV, and less than twenty-four hours later we headed to the Music City BMX National in Nashville, Tennessee.

As we puttered along in our new (old) RV, I couldn't help but feel overcome with gratitude. We had recently sold our home and nearly sixty percent of our belongings to move into a single-wide. Yet there I was—hand in hand with my soulmate, listening to my two beautiful daughters' delightful nonsense, surrounded by the two dogs I'd dreamed of having since I was a little girl. The entire day smelled of good fortune.

That weekend, Carly won her first National! She was met at the finish line by Wilbur and Opie.

I cannot put into words how much Wilbur and Opie relished the RV! They had their own pullout bed, and absolutely loved being on the road with us. Anytime they'd see us loading up the RV, they'd lie in front of the entrance to ensure that they wouldn't be left behind.

The summer of 2016 was one of the best of our lives. We turned BMX trips into mini vacations, and Wilbur and Opie were able to experience the ocean together. One of my favorite memories was watching Carly and Heidi cover the dogs with sand, turning them into "mermen." I loved witnessing the contagious joy that Wilbur and Opie brought to everyone around them. By that fall, Carly had earned the BMX sponsorship she had dreamed of, and she subsequently signed with DK Bicycles.

*Wilbur and Opie curled up in the RV after a day of fun.*

*Saint Bernards are such a special breed–patient, gentle, and eager to please, even when our requests make little sense to them.*

One of my favorite benefits of owning a dog is that they motivate you to be more active. I had never really enjoyed winter, but it was Wilbur and Opie's favorite season. It made sense because Saint Bernards were originally bred and trained to rescue travelers buried under snow or trapped in blizzards. I don't believe that there's anything a Saint Bernard loves more than snow.

I quickly discovered that when you buy the appropriate clothing, winter is truly enjoyable! No matter the weather, we explored our land every day. When the days got shorter and our schedules filled up, we'd put on our headlamps and walk under the stars. It was so still you could hear a pin drop, and that quiet brought me a kind of peace I can't describe.

Thanks to Wilbur and Opie we learned to enjoy the cold, and even began to look forward to frigid temperatures that would allow us to ice skate on the pond.

*Top left: Wilbur trotting faithfully behind me as I ice skate across our frozen pond. Top right: Wilbur and Heidi savoring the ice together. Bottom left: Wilbur sharing a moment of affection with Brian. Bottom right: Opie grinning ear to ear, reveling in the fresh, powdery snow.*

There was no denying that the trailer was cold! It was so cold, in fact, that the locks would freeze overnight, and each morning we had to use a hairdryer to thaw them out. Wilbur and Opie used to look at us with pleading eyes, wondering what was taking so long to let them outside!

Brian finished our home plans over the winter, but finding someone to pour the foundation in the springtime proved impossible. Everyone was booked solid, and our floor plan was considerably more complex than those of the average house in our area, so contractors were reluctant to assume the task.

Time moved on. Carly excelled on her bike, and seeing her dreams take shape inspired Brian to bring Heidi's dream of owning a horse to life. We found a twelve-year-old Haflinger named Joey. We boarded him at a farm just two miles away and purchased a small horse trailer so that Heidi could ride him on our land. Wilbur, Opie, and Joey quickly became the best of friends. It was pure bliss, running behind Heidi with the dogs and hearing her giggles of delight.

*Left: Carly taking a turn on Joey, while Joey gives Wilbur a gentle nudge to pick up the pace. Right: Carly and Heidi riding Joey together, with Wilbur and Opie close behind.*

Wilbur and Opie were always eager for the next adventure, whatever it might be. They loved following behind Joey on the trails, and sharing carrots with him, but another activity that Opie especially looked forward to was kayaking on the river with us. I remember visiting a local kayaking spot where the woman working was adamant that we'd never get "that monster" into a kayak. She was condescending and even followed us to the drop-off point just to witness the chaos she was sure would unfold. I'll never forget grinning deviously at her as Opie hopped right in, and we drifted down the river high on life.

*Opie and me, radiating joy as we float down the river together.*

Our land was glorious, but we were definitely getting anxious to have space again. Wilbur and Opie loved the trailer and being in such close quarters. On the other hand, the four of us could do without the mice scurrying around in the walls, the mushrooms growing in the carpet, and the plants sprouting from the sink.

Wilbur weighed 140 pounds, and Opie had reached 180. It was impossible to keep up with the dog hair. Since we didn't have access to city water, we had to haul water every day. It was inconvenient for us, but something Wilbur and Opie looked forward to—they got to ride in "the big red truck!"

The single-wide had only a 1,200-gallon cistern. We had to use water sparingly and would often run out. The dogs were usually bathed in the creek. We didn't realize just how bad the trailer smelled until years later, after we had moved out.

We had to run three window A/C units at all times to keep Wilbur and Opie cool, which created a constant hurricane of hair. We found ourselves dining out most of the time. The idea of dog hair in our food was unappetizing, and with almost no counter space and Brian using the tiny kitchen table as his desk, preparing meals in the trailer was hardly practical.

At night, I'd often wake up with a jolt and grab Brian's arm. "What was that?!" I'd whisper.

"Opie laid down," he'd reply.

The entire trailer would shake as he tried to get comfortable.

I reminded the girls that when you're a happy person, you can be happy anywhere. I told them to embrace our hardships and regard them as a challenge. One of my favorite quotes became, *"Pursuing your dreams is living a few years of your life like most people won't, so you can spend the rest of your life like most people can't."* I did everything in my power to keep my family happy and used humor as a coping mechanism.

We started many fun traditions while living in the single-wide. We'd celebrate Wilbur and Opie's birthdays and bake them special cakes. On Valentine's Day, I'd put on my boldest red lipstick and give the pups a kiss on the whites of their muzzles, making sure to snap some photos. At Halloween, Brian would carve me a Saint Bernard dog jack-o-lantern. I'd collect snow from the first snowfall and make "doggie" ice cream. During the holidays we'd take Wilbur and Opie to see the Easter Bunny and Santa. (Wilbur and Opie always stole the show!)

*Wilbur posing with the Saint Bernard jack-o-lantern that Brian carved for me.*

At Christmas we wore matching pajamas and took family photos. Wilbur always looked at me as though he were appalled at having to wear pajamas, but we couldn't get Opie's on fast enough! I've never seen a dog more excited about wearing clothes. We even bought a giant inflatable Saint Bernard to display at Christmas and decorated gingerbread trailers.

*Our giant inflatable Saint Bernard in front of the single-wide.*

We also started a "happiness jar" to remind ourselves that even on the hardest days, there's always something good to be found. Each day, the four of us would individually write down something positive, a moment that made us smile or something we were grateful for, and place it in the jar. Then, on New Year's Day, we'd read all the notes together as a family, reflecting on the joy and gratitude that filled our year.

By April of 2018, the trailer had deteriorated into a dwelling that most would consider uninhabitable. The ceiling had partially collapsed. The majority of the blinds had long since been torn from the windows, which were now covered with blankets and affixed with duct tape. Mice had infested every available paper product including paper towels, toilet paper, tissues, cotton balls, and had even taken up residence in our clean towels. They had also overtaken our kitchen cabinets, and every time I tried to cook, I'd find mouse droppings in the pots and pans, which I had to thoroughly sterilize before using. Brian had made a futile attempt to seal out the mice by discharging numerous cans of spray foam insulation in every crack and crevice, visible or not.

The heating bills for the trailer were horrendous. None of our previous homes had come with such outrageous utility bills, especially for a trailer kept at a constant, tooth-chattering, sixty degrees.

Two years after living in the trailer, with no option but to move forward, we finally broke ground. At best our move-in date was already two years behind what we had originally anticipated, and little did we know that our time in the trailer would double before it was over.

We subcontracted the foundation, drywall, plumbing, HVAC, and some of the roofing, but we physically completed every other aspect of our home ourselves. Brian framed the entire house with the help of my brother who had never even used a circular saw. Without any machinery, Brian and my brother built all of the interior and exterior walls of our home on the ground. Then, the three of us physically raised them by hand, with occasional help from our kids and any friends that we could rally.

There simply weren't enough hours in the day to handle the workload that we faced, and we therefore got very little sleep. The longer we were in the trailer the more elaborate our house plans became. It was a massive undertaking, and though the years have flown by, we still look back and say: *We don't know how we did it.*

A year passed, and we were still spending every free moment on the construction of our home. Carly began to experience lower back pain, and an MRI revealed that she had an L5 stress fracture in her spine. She received the disheartening news that she would have to wear a back brace twenty-four hours a day for the duration of the summer, during which any strenuous physical activity would be prohibited.

I mentioned to Brian that one of my coworker's friends had Saint Bernard puppies available! The pups were located just over the river in Kentucky. A puppy felt like the perfect remedy for almost anything, and I wanted to lift Carly's spirits. Wilbur was six years old, and sadly the life expectancy of a Saint Bernard is only eight to ten years. Brian and I often worried about the inevitable day we'd have to say goodbye. We feared that when the time came, Opie would lose the will to live without another canine companion. My coworker put me in touch with the breeder, and I reached out to schedule a time that afternoon to come "look" at the puppies.

Because so many Saint Bernards were available in shelters, many people questioned our decision to go through breeders. However, our unfortunate experience with Otis had left us feeling hesitant about rescuing—especially after some had gone so far as to suggest we surrender him. We were genuinely concerned about the unknown challenges that we might be bringing into our home.

When we arrived, the puppy we had requested to see had seemingly vanished! We searched everywhere and eventually found him inside of a cabinet, tucked beneath a fish tank! All of us agreed that his ornery personality seemed like a perfect match for our family.

We named him Huckleberry. The only thing better than having two Saint Bernards... was having three! Imagine that— three Saint Bernards in a single-wide trailer! And to think, my parents once said my childhood home was too small for even one.

Huckleberry adored Wilbur but tormented Opie. Sweet and docile, Opie tolerated Huckleberry's antics with remarkable patience. Opie seemed a little distraught over having to share "his" Wilbur. To reassure him, we started feeding Opie first to show him that he was still loved, but we later learned that was a mistake. Dogs are pack animals, and when their place in the hierarchy is unclear, they can become confused and anxious. We found that feeding, greeting, and rewarding them in pack order helped create a sense of stability and peace. We continued to learn.

*Top to bottom: Huckleberry, Wilbur, and Opie.*

Carly and Huckleberry formed an instant bond. He was just what the doctor ordered. I had never seen a dog that loved water as much as Huckleberry. He delighted in hurling himself theatrically through the air and leaping from the banks of our pond with a mighty splash. He had a larger-than-life personality and brought us much laughter.

*Left: Carly receiving Huckleberry's gentle, healing love. Right: Huckleberry riding on Heidi's back like a baby koala.*

Summer faded to autumn yet again, and Carly was cleared to get back on her bike. We braced ourselves for another winter in the trailer while Brian and I continued working tirelessly on our home. The two of us, along with the dogs, spent many hours wading through our icy creek, gathering creek rocks by hand to build the hearths for our fireplaces. The dogs became our constant companions at the construction site, never straying far from my side.

I remember one particular incident in which I, while helping Brian carry a piece of subfloor up a ladder, lost my balance and fell off backwards. I landed directly on my pile of Saint Bernards, who upon impact eagerly attacked me with slobbery kisses. Had it not been for them, I most likely would've been injured.

In February of 2020, when Wilbur was seven, we had just finished watching the Chiefs defeat the 49ers in Super Bowl LIV. We let the dogs out one final time before heading to bed. When Wilbur came back inside, we quickly realized that something was wrong. He was foaming at the mouth and he couldn't seem to get comfortable. He kept extending his chest and seemed to be in pain.

I had devoted countless hours to reading everything I could about Saint Bernards, absorbing as much information as possible. I learned that Gastric Dilatation and Volvulus (GDV)—commonly known as bloat—was a frequent and often deadly condition in the breed. Without immediate medical intervention, it is almost always fatal. In GDV, the abdomen fills with air, the stomach twists, and blood supply to vital organs, including the heart, is abruptly cut off.

I looked at Brian in alarm and shouted, "I think his stomach twisted! We've got to go NOW!" Racing to our car we sped to the emergency vet at 120 miles per hour. We had phoned the vet to inform him that we were en route, and upon our arrival they took Wilbur back immediately. It was confirmed that Wilbur's stomach had twisted, and emergency surgery was required or death was imminent. I recall the vet tech coming in with paperwork and explaining the estimated costs. Brian cut her off, "I don't care how much it costs! Just save him!"

Brian and I returned home and anxiously waited by the phone until receiving the news that the surgery was a success! The vet explained that prior to his taking X-rays, he had been reasonably confident that GDV wasn't the culprit; the condition is usually excruciatingly painful, and Wilbur had remained unusually calm and cooperative before and after the procedure.

Wilbur would need to stay at the pet hospital for forty-eight hours, but we were permitted to visit him. The next morning, the vet called and told me that Wilbur was doing well, but that they couldn't get him to empty his bladder. I exclaimed, "I can get him to! I'm on my way!"

Sure enough, as soon as I arrived, Wilbur relaxed and emptied his bladder.

Two days later, Brian brought Wilbur home. I was working a waitressing shift to help cover the cost of Wilbur's surgery. Opie and

Huckleberry had spent the past two days frantically searching for him, and they were overjoyed when he returned. Wilbur was in immense pain and was clearly sore. He had staples that ran down the entire length of his abdomen. We weren't sure if he would ever make a full recovery. The moment I came home from work, his tail wagged for the first time since surgery.

To our amazement, Wilbur bounced back faster than anyone expected. We were convinced that it was because he genuinely loved his life "in the holler."

The cause of bloat is unknown. We had consistently followed every recommended precaution. We never allowed the dogs to exercise for at least an hour before or after eating. We used slow-feeder bowls placed on the ground and divided their meals into smaller portions throughout the day. Despite all of these efforts, Wilbur still wasn't spared.

Our vet suggested giving Wilbur two extra-strength Gas-X tablets daily as a preventative. If you own a Saint Bernard or any deep-chested dog prone to bloat, I highly encourage you to look into laparoscopic gastropexy as a preventive option, if it's available in your area.

By March of 2020, nearly FOUR years after moving into the trailer, we had finally reached our limit. Our house was only about sixty percent complete, and while we knew that moving in meant living in a construction zone, we couldn't spend another moment in the single-wide. A friend called and asked if we'd sell the trailer to him for $1,500—and promised that he would haul it away himself. Without hesitation, we said YES! We packed up our clothes, left everything else behind, and walked away to a fresh start.

Not long after moving into our new home, Opie began limping. We made him an appointment with his veterinarian, and we were informed that he had a torn cranial cruciate ligament (CCL). His injury would require surgery.

There was only one specialist in our region who could perform tibial plateau leveling osteotomy (TPLO) surgery on such a large dog. With Wilbur's emergency surgery behind us and another major procedure ahead, it was shaping up to be a very expensive year—but our Saints were family. They were worth every penny.

Opie's procedure entailed cutting and rotating the top portion of the shin bone to eliminate reliance on the cranial cruciate ligament, with subsequent stabilization of the knee joint using a plate and screws.

We were assured that Opie would leave in better shape than when he arrived. We scheduled his surgery for the following week, and we were hopeful that soon Opie would be back to his old self.

The procedure went smoothly, but I nearly burst into tears when we went to pick him up. He could barely walk and blood was oozing from his incision. What we were told during the consultation didn't align with the reality in front of us. The operation turned out to be a significantly more invasive procedure than we had been led to believe.

It was 2020, and of course due to COVID many places were understaffed. It appeared that the young veterinary technician who had answered our questions during the consultation was lacking in sufficient knowledge or experience.

We were initially advised that Opie's recovery would take two weeks; in reality he would be confined to a cage for two to three months. It was heartbreaking to hear him howl whenever we were forced to leave him behind when going for walks or swimming at our pond. We did our best to comfort him with extra cuddles and special treats like marrow bones, but still he seemed very depressed.

The twelve weeks felt incredibly long, but Opie was overjoyed when he was finally cleared and could join in again on our adventures. Less than a week after being cleared, Opie tore the CCL in his other leg.

After researching the treatment protocol, I was upset to discover that dogs who tear one CCL have a forty to sixty percent chance of tearing the other. This risk is even higher in larger dogs.

Brian and I began searching online for an alternative treatment. We had no intention of putting Opie through another twelve weeks of misery. We came across the website of a company called Animal Ortho Care, and we were intrigued by their success stories. They made custom braces for animals as an alternative to surgery. Brian and I agreed that it was worth a shot.

The company sent us a casting kit to create a mold of Opie's leg, which we were instructed to return upon completion so that a custom brace could be fabricated. Opie held perfectly still while we made the mold, seeming to understand that we were trying to help him.

*Left: The joy Opie felt after being cleared from his surgery. Right: The mold of Opie's leg we made to send to Animal Ortho Care.*

Opie wore the brace continuously, except while sleeping at night. We gradually increased his activity, and within a month he was confidently running and playing again. After ten months, Opie no longer needed the brace at all. Remarkably, the leg that we had rehabbed with the brace fared much better than the leg that had undergone surgery.

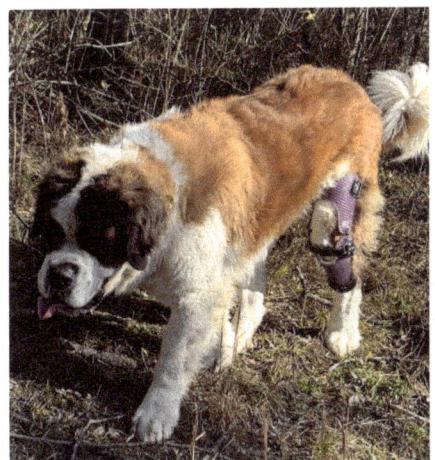 

*Left: Opie confidently walking in his brace, thrilled to join our adventures again. Right: Opie happily wearing his brace—he knew it helped him and was excited for us to put it on. He even swam in it!*

Brian and I felt incredibly proud that we had helped Opie avoid another operation. Our veterinarian considered his recovery to be a success story and even gave us the opportunity to speak with other clients who were exploring alternatives to surgery for their dogs. Brian and I gladly agreed to help several families make molds for their dogs' torn CCLs. All of those with whom we spoke were successful in rehabilitating their pets.

In 2020, the pandemic forced Carly to scale back on competitions, causing her to lose momentum in her pursuit of becoming a BMX champion. In 2021, Carly met her now-fiancé, Braydon, and they motivated one another to recommit to their personal goals.

Over the past several years, Brian and I had been so focused on building the house that we rarely had the chance to watch Carly compete in person. We promised her that if she stayed committed to her training, we would accompany her to Tulsa, Oklahoma, that November to watch her compete in the Grand Nationals. The Grand Nationals, which are annually held over Thanksgiving in Tulsa, are considered to be the most significant competition of the year in North American BMX. Carly did her part by putting in consistent hard work throughout the year leading up to the event.

When November arrived, we told Carly how proud we were of her effort and began planning our trip. But just as the excitement was building, something unexpected happened. At only two years of age, Huckleberry began vomiting and refused to eat. Concerned, we took him to the vet, who quickly performed an X-ray and discovered a piece of marrow bone lodged in his digestive tract. Our vet explained that while surgery would be necessary, it was a routine procedure and nothing to worry about. We kissed our sweet "Huckles" goodbye and told him we'd be back soon.

Shortly after Brian and I arrived home, I heard Brian on the phone with Huckleberry's vet. He asked Brian how many times Huckleberry had previously undergone surgery to which Brian answered, "Only when he was neutered."

Our veterinarian, who had been practicing animal medicine for over forty years, was perplexed by what he saw and remarked that he had never seen anything like it. He told us that when he opened Huckleberry up, his internal organs were covered with adhesions, which are abnormal bands of scar tissue that can cause organs that are normally separate to stick together. He was unable to distinguish where one organ ended and another began.

Although he successfully removed the bone fragment, he said a dog Huckleberry's size should have had no problem in passing it without medical intervention. The presence of such extensive internal scarring was deeply concerning. Our vet couldn't offer any guarantees about how long Huckleberry might live or what his quality of life would be.

We picked Huckleberry up the next day, not knowing what the future would hold. We spent every waking moment by his side. He was clearly unwell, but he never stopped wagging his tail.

Our veterinarian told us that once Huckleberry had a normal bowel movement, he would feel more confident that everything inside was functioning properly. Two days after the surgery, Huckleberry "did his business," and we let out a huge collective sigh of relief! Things seemed to be heading in the right direction!

But two weeks later and three days before we were supposed to leave for Tulsa, Huckleberry once again stopped eating and began vomiting. We returned to our vet who administered Barium to Huckleberry to determine if there was still a blockage—which there wasn't. There was the possibility that gas could be causing the symptoms.

Our veterinarian sent us home with anti-vomiting medication and suggested we try taking him for a walk. It was dark and thirty-one degrees outside, so we bundled up, grabbed our flashlights, and hoped for the best.

The next morning, Huckleberry refused everything that we tried to feed him. We were starting to feel panicked, because we knew we couldn't break our promise to Carly by missing the Grand Nationals. We were torn as to what we should do.

I spent hours searching online and messaged Huckleberry's vet asking if he thought that intussusception might be a possibility. Intussusception is a serious medical condition in which one part of the intestine slides into an adjacent part of the intestine. The condition can block the passage of food. The vet stated that it could be the problem, but that the only way to find out would be for him to perform exploratory surgery.

We mutually agreed that we would give it one more day. If we could get Huckleberry to eat before we headed to Tulsa that following morning, my mother-in-law would tend to Wilbur, Opie, and Huckleberry while we were away. If he continued to refuse food she would stay with Wilbur and Opie while we took Huckleberry to the vet for his surgery. If we opted for surgery, our vet assured us that he would care for Huckleberry during his recovery, allowing us to keep our promise and be there in Tulsa to support Carly.

We held our breath as we offered Huckleberry chicken and steak the following morning. We exchanged somber glances when he wouldn't eat. We kissed Huckleberry goodbye as he headed to the vet with Brian. I was filled with uncertainty, wondering whether or not we had made the right decision.

Carly had flown to Tulsa the day before to take part in her practice session. Heidi, Braydon (Carly's boyfriend), Brian and I set out for Tulsa by car. Two hours into our drive, Huckleberry's veterinarian called. Brian put his phone on speaker so that we could all listen.

"I have Huckleberry open on the table, and I'm so very sorry..." My heart sank as he continued... "He has so many new adhesions that I can't even see my incision from two weeks ago. I believe that the humane thing to do at this point is euthanasia." Tearfully, we agreed, fully aware that we had done everything possible to save him. We requested that Huckleberry be cremated so we could bring him home with us. We hung up the phone and started sobbing.

We knew that Carly would be especially heartbroken, but there was no choice but to tell her. Given the timing, we worried about how it would affect her ability to compete. I tried to comfort her, telling her that she now had a guardian angel watching over her. Deep down, I truly believe that Huckleberry had beautifully served the purpose for which God had intended him, which was to be there for Carly as she recovered from her back injury.

The next day was Thanksgiving, and while we were in no mood to celebrate, we were mindful of the fact that we had much for which to be grateful. We decided to have our Thanksgiving dinner at Cracker Barrel. The hostess seated us at a table in the far corner of the restaurant. Our conversation centered around memories of Huckleberry.

Just as I had remarked that I felt sad over having never taken Huckleberry to the ocean, Carly's eyes lit up and she exclaimed,

"Mom! Look, on the wall behind you!" I could hardly believe my eyes! There was a painting of a Saint Bernard, with the same markings as Huckleberry, watching over a little girl at the ocean. At the bottom of the painting was the title, *Guarding*. We all got goosebumps and took it as a sign from above.

The memory of the entire trip is a blur, and truthfully I can't even remember how Carly performed. Returning home to only two dogs was difficult. It seemed as though Wilbur and Opie had presumed that Huckleberry had been traveling with us. There was an unexpected package on our porch. I opened it and was surprised to see the painting from Cracker Barrel. Carly's boyfriend, Braydon, had surprised us and ordered a print on eBay. We immediately hung it in our foyer.

We made sure to give Wilbur and Opie plenty of extra affection and love. I even bought them hoodies with my face on them—and got a matching one for myself with their faces on it. We took them along with us to pick out a Christmas tree in the "big red truck." We ordered a custom-made stuffed animal that looked just like Huckleberry from an online company called Cuddle Clones. Carly got a tattoo of a huckleberry branch on the inside of her forearm to honor our sweet friend.

*Left: The painting "Guarding" by British artist Arthur John Elsley. Right: Huckleberry's markings bore an uncanny resemblance to the Saint Bernard depicted in the painting.*

*Left: Wilbur, Opie, and me in our matching hoodies. Right: The replica we had made of Huckleberry and Carly's tattoo.*

Around the time we lost Huckleberry, Budweiser released a holiday beer can featuring a Saint Bernard dog wearing a Christmas wreath. In my entire life, I've probably had no more than fifteen alcoholic drinks, but I *had* to have one of those cans as a keepsake.

I sent Brian out on a beer run, and when he got home, I couldn't believe it—there wasn't a single Saint Bernard can in the pack. I told him I was going to exchange it, and he laughed. "There's no way they're going to let you return an open twelve-pack," he said.

But I was determined.

Heidi tagged along, curious to see what would happen. When we walked into the liquor store, the woman behind the counter gave me a look and said, "Please tell me you're not returning beer! I don't think I've ever seen anyone do that in my life."

I explained my mission to her, and why it meant so much to me. To my surprise, she didn't just let me exchange it—she jumped right in to help. The three of us—her, Heidi, and me—tore through more than ten twelve-packs before realizing the Saint Bernard cans were only in the twenty-four packs.

When I finally checked out, I told her she'd made me the happiest I'd been since losing Huckleberry. I suggested that if anyone else came in looking for those cans, she could tell them where to find them.

She smiled and winked. "I don't think there's going to be anyone else like you," she said.

She truly made my night. And yes, we did drink a beer for Huckleberry. That's one of the fifteen I've had in my life, and it tasted like a toast to sweet "Huckles."

We had all come to love the joy and chaos that came with owning three Saint Bernards, but our hearts still needed time to heal. One of the things I had cherished most about my trio was how instinctively they protected me. Whenever a car came down our road, all three would sit firmly at my feet, placing themselves between me and the approaching vehicle, standing guard until I gave them the all-clear.

It always made me smile when we'd run into Opie—the man who had sold us our trailer. With pride in his voice, he'd tell his passengers, "You see that dog right there? He's named after me."

I was feeling the weight of Huckleberry's absence, yet spending time with Wilbur and Opie brought me back to my childhood memory. They reminded me of the two Saint Bernards I had encountered when I was twelve years old. Curious to know their names, I reached out on Facebook to the mother of the family for whom I once babysat, hoping that she could contact her friend. Although she said that they had lost touch over the years, she did provide me with the friend's name. When I typed his name into Facebook's search bar, I was surprised to discover that Brian's aunt was listed as a mutual friend. She was able to connect the two of us, and I was elated to learn that their names had been **Norman** and **Stanley**.

I shared with their owner how much I would have loved to hang a framed photo of his two dogs in our home. Unfortunately, back in the 1990s, smartphones weren't around to capture every moment. Sadly, Norman and Stanley's owner had no such photos. Still, I was delighted to learn their names.

Brian and I continued to work together diligently on our home. I had come to the conclusion that the addition of a designated dog shower would be necessary. I began searching online for unique shower tiles. I stumbled upon a website that offered handmade metallic tiles featuring various breeds, but they did not offer a Saint Bernard.

I sent the company a message asking if they'd consider creating a custom Saint Bernard tile. The owner replied promptly and enthusiastically agreed. I then messaged, *I noticed that the dog tiles on your site have names. Would you consider naming the Saint Bernard tile after one of my dogs? I have a Wilbur and an Opie.*

The owner responded back, *So not only do you want me to make you custom tiles, but now you want me to name them after your dogs?*

I replied, *yep,* with a smiley-face emoji.

Even through text, the tone was lighthearted and friendly. When the tiles were finally added to the website, I was thrilled to see that they had been named *Opie.*

In April of 2022, we were on our way home from a family vacation. Brian was driving, and I was absentmindedly scrolling through Facebook when I suddenly stopped in my tracks. A friend had shared a post featuring the most adorable Saint Bernard puppy I'd ever seen—and he was up for sale. The breeder had requested that whoever purchased him would at least consider showing him on the dog show circuit, as she believed he had strong potential. I turned to Brian and exclaimed, "Look at this puppy! I really think he might be the one!"

Just five days after our twelve-hour drive home from Florida, Brian and I again packed up the car and made a sixteen-hour trip to Pennsylvania and back to bring home *Augustus the Magnificent* or "Gus", as we called him. Wilbur was delighted, but Opie gave us a look that clearly said, *You've got to be kidding me.*

Our dogs adjusted quickly, in part because we were much more intentional about reinforcing their place within the pack. Wilbur was now nine, and Opie was six. The large age gap between our boys hadn't been planned—but then, we hadn't expected to lose Huckleberry so young.

Brian and I kept our word to the breeder, and enrolled Gus in conformation training, which is designed to prepare dogs and their handlers for the show ring. We attended several shows and were captivated not only by the Saint Bernards but by the wide variety of breeds that truly embodied their breed standards. Every one of them was a stunning animal. We met some friendly and authentic people at the shows, but quickly decided that the show world was not our scene. Gus was perfectly content spending his days on our land, chasing vultures soaring overhead and joyfully trying to catch water striders in the creek.

*With that little face, bringing Gus home was the only option.*

In the fall of 2022, Heidi's boyfriend, Eli—whom she had started dating earlier that year—agreed to take care of our animals while we were away on a family trip. She left him detailed instructions on how to care for her cat, Fernando. But when she checked in later that week, she discovered that Eli had misunderstood and was filling the wrong bowl with kibble—one that held nearly ten times what Fernando would normally eat. When she brought the mistake to his attention, Eli exclaimed, "Well he's been eating it all," which we knew was impossible.

After returning home we discovered that Gus was the "cat food bandit." We always set Fernando's food on the other side of the fence so that he could eat in peace without the dogs bothering him. Gus had figured out how to climb over the fence and help himself to Fernando's dinner. We corrected Gus multiple times, and he clearly knew that what he was doing was wrong, but he was apparently unable to control himself. We had to put a stop to the problem, because Fernando obviously needed to eat, and we didn't want Gus getting hurt.

Brian installed an electric fence around the area where Fernando liked to relax and eat. That night, with help from the baby monitor we used to keep an eye on the dogs, Brian and I watched Gus as he wrestled with temptation. He'd get up, sniff the air, catch a whiff of Fernando's food, then lie back down, clearly aware that he wasn't allowed to eat it. This went on for two solid hours. Eventually, his self-control gave out. He managed to climb over the fence, and I swear I could see him grinning. Just as he was about to devour the food, he got zapped, and leaped back over the fence like a gazelle. That was the last time Gus ever tried to eat Fernando's food.

In the summer of 2023, Brian and I arrived home from grocery shopping, and instantly knew that Wilbur had bloated again. His stomach was three times its normal size, and he was clearly in discomfort.

We dropped our grocery bags and rushed to the car, heading straight to the emergency vet because it was a Saturday. What we already suspected was quickly confirmed. Fortunately, the emergency gastropexy that was performed three years earlier had done its job and prevented his stomach from twisting.

The situation was still an emergency that required prompt veterinary treatment, because even if the stomach doesn't twist, the gas inside can compress blood vessels, reducing blood flow to vital organs. The veterinarian immediately inserted a needle through Wilbur's abdominal wall to relieve gas. Wilbur was then placed under anesthesia, and a tube was passed through his mouth and into his stomach to release the remaining gas. There are emergency bloat kits available online, but I can't imagine attempting that kind of procedure on a conscious dog.

Wilbur stayed overnight at the pet hospital to receive intravenous fluids. Meanwhile, Opie and Gus searched frantically for him. Wilbur was ten years old, and although he pulled through, his recovery was difficult. I couldn't bear to think about the day that we would lose him.

In those quiet, anxious days after bringing him home, I found myself searching for anything that might bring comfort when that day eventually came. While scrolling through Facebook, I came across a page for Heart of Heaven Farm and Gifts, a small business offering a unique and touching service. Customers can send in a sample of their dog's fur, which is then blended with wool to create a custom needle-felted replica of their beloved pet. The end product is masterfully done. I ordered one of both Wilbur and Opie, knowing that someday I would want something tangible to hold on to.

We made it another eight months until Wilbur bloated again. The same procedure from the previous episode was performed, and the vet prescribed Metoclopramide to help move food more efficiently through his stomach and intestines. She recommended administering the medication for the remainder of Wilbur's life and suggested exploratory surgery in an effort to determine the root cause of his gastrointestinal issues.

Wilbur was extremely weak, suffering from severe diarrhea, and needed Brian's and my help just to get up from the floor. We loved him dearly, and we didn't think it was fair—or even reasonable—to put our aging pet through such a high-risk operation. It seemed to us that the medication was actually delaying his recovery. So Brian and I stopped giving Wilbur the drug and watched closely for any changes, good or bad. Almost immediately after we stopped, Wilbur's diarrhea ceased, and his strength began to return.

Brian and I agreed that no matter how much time Wilbur had left, we wanted his life to be lived to the fullest and with as much quality and joy as possible. Two months later, we celebrated his eleventh birthday, and I baked him his favorite pumpkin cake.

We were enjoying a wonderful summer. Heidi and I had started competing together with considerable success in mother/daughter tennis Nationals across the country. Carly had turned pro in BMX and was riding for Huffy Bicycles (@carlyracesbmx). Through it all, we had Brian's full support as he continued working on a multitude of projects related to the construction of our new home.

Wilbur and Opie were slowing down significantly, and often scolded Gus whenever he tried to engage them in play. We thought that a possible solution might be to bring home another puppy so that Gus, who was only two, would have a lively companion with whom to play.

We had been planning to accompany Carly to a BMX National in Nashville, Tennessee, and it just so happened that a friend of a friend—living only forty minutes from the track—had a puppy ready for a new home. Heidi was thrilled; she had always wanted a Saint Bernard with a half mask like that of the available puppy. All of our previous Saint Bernards had full masks, meaning that they bore darker markings that symmetrically covered both sides of their face.

Our puppy "Arthur" had a dark patch covering one eye, while the other side of his face was white. We found it especially charming that one eye was framed by black eyelashes, and the other by white.

When we brought Arthur home, things didn't quite go as planned. Wilbur and Opie accepted him immediately; however, Arthur growled at Gus, and Gus, acting like a big baby, was terrified. If Arthur so much as brushed up against him, Gus would flee with his tail tucked between his legs. Arthur was definitely a more introverted puppy than what we had been used to. Part of that may have been because, whenever Arthur came near, Gus would get so jealous that he'd wedge himself between us.

From the very beginning, Arthur was obsessed with tennis balls. They brought him comfort, and he would even suck on them in his sleep like they were a pacifier. Playing fetch with us became our special way to bond with him—it was his absolute favorite pastime. Meanwhile, Gus looked on with obvious jealousy.

*Arthur, contentedly sucking on a tennis ball in his sleep.*

It was July 4, 2024. Carly and her boyfriend, Braydon, were attending a BMX National in Michigan. Heidi and her boyfriend, Eli, were at a fireworks show, while Brian and I spent the day swimming with our dogs in the pond. It was joyful and relaxing—a perfect summer day.

*From left to right: Wilbur, Opie, Arthur (with a huge grin!), and Gus heading to enjoy a day at the pond with Brian and me.*

The next evening, on my way home from a waitressing shift, Brian called to say that he didn't think Wilbur was feeling well. Wilbur had eaten all of his dinner, but was now panting, and clearly uncomfortable with gas. I told Brian that when I got home we would give Wilbur a warm bath and massage him in an attempt to make him comfortable. Wilbur found our touch to be soothing, and he seemed to relax. I sat by his side for the rest of the evening, gently stroking his fur.

The next morning, Wilbur seemed even more distressed. He refused to eat, and frequently stared into the woods. There had been so many times in the past when Wilbur seemed to be on his deathbed, yet he always pulled through—so I held onto hope that he would bounce back once again.

Heidi, Brian, and I accompanied Wilbur to the vet in "the big red truck." Carly was still away competing in Michigan. We wept as the vet gently told us that not only had Wilbur bloated for the fourth time, but that now there was fluid around his heart. The time that we had dreaded had come for Wilbur.

The vet stepped out to give us some private time with him. We FaceTimed Carly, who tearfully begged us to wait until she could get home. She insisted that she would leave Michigan immediately. We lovingly explained to her that Wilbur was in significant pain, and that it wouldn't be fair to prolong his suffering. Even as I write this, the pain remains fresh, and the tears still fall.

*"Once you have had a wonderful dog, a life without one is a life diminished." - Dean Koontz*

All of us were grieving. That included Opie, Gus, and Arthur, who had lost their alpha. We were especially concerned for Opie, because he and Wilbur had bonded deeply. Surprisingly, Gus took the loss harder than did Opie and showed signs of depression. He became lethargic, with a sadness in his eyes that was unmistakable. Gus was not only coming to terms with the loss of his leader, but was also adjusting to no longer being the youngest of the pack. In the past, whenever Wilbur was away at the vet for an extended time, the other dogs would frantically search for him. But this time, they didn't. It was as if they somehow understood what had happened.

*Left: Arthur gazing up at Wilbur shortly before we lost him—such big shoes for a little fella to fill. Right: Arthur offering comfort after Wilbur's passing.*

Having a four-month-old puppy helped us cope with Wilbur's death, but all of us were nonetheless grief-stricken. I was grateful that Arthur had been afforded six weeks alongside Wilbur, soaking up his wisdom. We knew that we needed to have some family fun that would help to lift our spirits. I suggested that we go kayaking on the nearby Whitewater River, and bring along Opie, Gus, and Arthur. Brian and I piled into the "big red truck" with the dogs, and Carly and Heidi drove separately. Gus joined Brian and me in a tandem kayak, Opie rode with Carly in another, and Arthur was in a kayak with Heidi. It was exactly the kind of healing our hearts needed. We were the talk of the river, wrapped in a radiant energy that in my heart felt like Wilbur's presence.

*Top left: 180-pound Opie floats down the river with Carly. Top right: Arthur rides with Heidi, experiencing kayaking for the first time. Bottom: Gus 'rocks the boat' after spotting a blue heron downstream.*

Two weeks after losing Wilbur, I took Opie, Gus, and Arthur for a morning walk. Walking through the woods with my dogs has always been a peaceful time for me to say my prayers. It was a cool morning for July, and I was enjoying watching the dogs play in an open field.

Suddenly, I heard Arthur begin yelping in pain. When I turned around, it looked like he was covered in burrs. But, as I rushed over, I realized that the "burrs" covering his fur were angry yellow jackets—and they began stinging me, as well. At sixty pounds, Arthur was too heavy for me to carry the half-mile back to our house. I had no choice but to sprint home as fast as I could; thankfully, the dogs followed close behind.

I began screaming for Brian, who was not yet clear on what had happened. I grabbed the hose and attempted to spray the yellow jackets off of Arthur. Hysterical and breathless, I hoisted Arthur into our SUV, while frantically telling Brian that we needed to get Arthur to the vet as quickly as possible. I was still removing yellow jackets from Arthur's fur as Brian raced toward the vet's office. Arthur was growing lethargic, and I feared that we might lose him.

The vet administered injections of both steroids and Benadryl, and he advised us to watch Arthur closely. When we got home, I was thrilled to see the first genuine sign of affection from Gus. He rushed over and licked Arthur as if he'd been anxiously awaiting his return.

On the following day, Arthur's elbow swelled to the size of a softball. The quantity and toxicity of the yellow jackets' venom caused the fluid-filled pocket around his elbow to rupture. The vet prescribed antibiotics, and Arthur made a full recovery. Thankfully, his size as a Saint Bernard puppy likely made the difference between life and death. A smaller dog probably wouldn't have survived. The incident soon faded from our minds and we didn't give it much more thought.

Three months later, Gus remained indifferent toward Arthur, exhibiting no real interest in playing with him. I had lately been considering getting yet another puppy. Arthur had been acquired as a playmate for Gus, but Gus showed no desire to engage. I wanted Arthur to have a playmate.

Facebook had clearly become a budget minefield for my wallet; for as I scrolled, an irresistibly cute, white-faced Saint Bernard puppy suddenly appeared in my feed. The family who had been in the process of adopting him had encountered an unexpected financial hardship. The puppy was now available to other interested buyers. I showed the pup to Brian, hoping that he would say no to my folly, but the puppy was soooooo adorable that Brian was smitten.

I showed the puppy to Carly, and she instantly pleaded with me to bring him home. I reminded Carly that Brian, Heidi, and I would be heading to Florida in three weeks for the Mother/Daughter Clay Court Nationals. Not to be dissuaded, Carly promised that she would stay home to take care of the new puppy. Brian and I talked it over, and we eventually decided to surprise our girls with the puppy. It was something we hadn't done since we'd gotten Otis. We placed our deposit, and for the first time ever, the puppy would be delivered to us from Florida—no long drive required. We would name him Linus.

*The photos of Linus that I stumbled upon on Facebook. How could anyone say no to that face?*

Two days before Linus was scheduled to arrive, Arthur's elbow became swollen again. We hoped that the swelling was due to a spider bite or a wasp sting. Because Arthur was eating and behaving normally, we gave him some Benadryl before putting him to bed. By the next morning however, Arthur's leg had swollen to four times its normal size. It was a Saturday, as luck would have it, which meant that a trip to the emergency vet would be necessary.

Upon our arrival, Arthur was running a 105-degree fever, due to a severely infected, abscessed leg. The bacterium *E. coli* was the likely culprit, given how rapidly the swelling was spreading. The original bee-sting-related infection from that past July, which had caused the rupture, may never have fully cleared from his system. Arthur was sedated, and the abscess was lanced and drained of nearly two-thirds of a liter of fluid.

The vet tech explained that it would cost an additional $500 to run a culture to identify the specific bacteria causing the infection, and that we could expect the results in six days. Brian loves our dogs as deeply as I do. His devotion to our animals is one of his most endearing qualities. Our regular vet, who knows us and our animals well, has never taken advantage of that devotion. But in emergency settings, where there's no established relationship, you can sometimes feel pressured into extra tests simply because you're scared and vulnerable.

Brian was just about to sign the paperwork authorizing further testing when something made me hesitate. I've learned to trust my intuition, which I firmly believe is the Holy Spirit whispering guidance. I spoke up: "Hold on a second. If we don't have the results for six days, what's the point? By then, Arthur will either be cured or... well, he won't. As long as the antibiotic covers a broad enough spectrum to treat it, I don't care what its scientific name is."

So, we opted against the additional testing.

Complicating matters, the vet told us that Arthur wouldn't be able to meet the new puppy until he had fully healed. His recovery could take up to six weeks. Brian, Heidi, and I were scheduled to head out of town the following week for the Mother/Daughter Clay Court Nationals. I would have backed out of the tournament, but Heidi's plane ticket and our hotel reservation, both non-refundable, had already been booked.

I had wanted Linus's arrival to be a big surprise for the girls, but now it was turning into an "all hands on deck" situation. Due to his infection and the fact that his wound was still actively draining, Arthur would need to be crated for a month and only allowed out on a leash. He couldn't be around Linus because the bacteria from his abscess could make the little pup sick. I was feeling overwhelmed.

When Brian and I arrived home, the first thing out of Heidi's mouth was, "Oh my gosh! Aren't you glad we didn't get that puppy after all? That would've been a nightmare!"

My eyes widened and my brows lifted, and tucking my lips in I broke the news to my girls. "Well, Heidi... he arrives tomorrow."

Carly and Heidi stared at each other in dumbfounded silence.

With Braydon's help and Carly keeping her word, by the grace of God, we successfully handled the situation.

Heidi and I ended up taking second place in our tournament and brought home the USTA silver ball.

The six weeks flew by faster than expected, and before long Arthur and Linus had become the best of friends. It was exactly what I had pictured. Gus still preferred sticking close to Opie, but every now and then he'd sneak off to play with the puppies.

Linus was absolutely adorable. He reminded me so much of Wilbur— even down to his scent. One of Wilbur's characteristic traits was the way he would tilt his head when you spoke to him, as if he were trying to understand. My heart melted when Linus began doing the same.

It was clear that Linus had spent his first ten weeks of life in a home with five little girls, because he was unbelievably gentle and sweet. He was a funny little character, always letting out a signature belch after every meal.

*Top left: Linus tilts his head reminding us of Wilbur. Top right: Arthur and Linus, just five months apart in age. Bottom: Opie, as if whispering to Linus, 'Let me tell you about our old pal Wilbur.'*

It brought me much joy to walk through our woods with four Saint Bernards leading the way—I never stopped smiling. I had spent countless hours training them so that they could roam off-leash and just be dogs, free and happy. We had significantly reduced our pace for Opie, as he tended to fall behind because of his age. Still, his favorite part of the day was going for a walk. Every week, I boiled chicken and liver as high-value treats to be used during our walks as reinforcement for our commands, making certain that their hard work (and mine) paid off.

*From front to back: Linus, Arthur, me, Gus, and Opie.*

On January 6, 2025, a date easy for me to remember since it's my birthday, I woke up to a great surprise. Fourteen inches of fresh, powdery snow had fallen overnight! I could imagine no better gift than being snowed-in with my family while watching our dogs romp and play joyfully together in the cold, deep, and delicate whiteness!

Since Carly and Braydon had left for Florida two days earlier so that Carly could train over the winter, they were disappointed to miss out on the fun.

Two months earlier, Opie had injured his paw pad, and because of his weight and the location of the wound, the healing process had been slow. He had to wear a boot on his front paw, which made it a burden for him to walk through the snow.

While we were playing in the snow, Opie's breathing suddenly deteriorated into labored, ragged, and clearly agonizing gasps. Shortly thereafter, Opie collapsed. Soon there was no breath… the color of Opie's gums and tongue had now become an alarming, sickening shade of blue. Believing the worst, I tried to comfort Heidi by telling her that at least Opie had passed while doing something that he loved; exploring our land and playing in the snow.

*Enjoying a day in the snow shortly before Opie's collapse.*

We were located halfway up a rather steep hill, so I asked Brian to get our tractor so that we could haul Opie's body back to the house.

While Brian was getting the tractor, I knelt beside Opie, gently massaging his chest, telling him how much we loved him, and what a good boy he was. Then, out of nowhere, he inhaled slowly and began to breathe!

When Brian returned with the tractor, he was stunned to see Opie alive, still lying in the snow but able to hold his head up. Brian and Eli lifted him gently onto the platform at the rear of the tractor. I rode with Opie, holding him close. We brought him inside, laid him in his bed, wrapped him in warm towels, and placed him near a heater. Within minutes of our arriving home, Opie was acting as though nothing had happened. He devoured a banana—his all-time favorite treat, and his expression seemed to question why we were looking at him so strangely.

I sat with Opie for over three hours; stroking his back, singing to him, and listening to his sweet snores. I was utterly stunned by what we had just witnessed. I truly believe that Wilbur had given Opie a little nudge and whispered, *You can't leave her on her birthday!*

The next day—and every day after—I'd look at Opie in disbelief, wondering, *How are you still here?* I began calling him my "miracle boy." After the incident, we began the practice of tucking him in each night, wrapping him snugly in blankets. When Gus, Arthur, and Linus saw Opie's new bedtime routine, they wanted the same. So every evening, I'd tuck them in one by one, from oldest to youngest, kissing each of their heads and telling them I loved them before turning out the light.

As soon as we managed to dig out from the snow, we scheduled an appointment with our veterinarian. They took chest X-rays, blood work, and a urinalysis, and everything was normal. We needed answers. We knew Opie would be nine the following month, but no matter how much time he had left, if there was anything we could do to improve his quality of life, he absolutely deserved it. We had watched him come back to life before our eyes! I was still in awe. It gave me chills just thinking about it. There was no explanation other than a miracle… and the power of love.

We scheduled an appointment with a canine cardiologist. Opie's EKG, echocardiogram, and blood pressure all came back normal. I felt a deep sense of gratification, believing that the healthy lifestyle and loving home we had given Opie had contributed to his remarkable recovery.

Opie was diagnosed with Laryngeal Paralysis which is "a condition in which the muscles and nerves that control the larynx stop working properly. This causes the airway to become partially blocked, making it difficult for the animal—usually a dog—to breathe, especially during exercise, excitement, or heat."

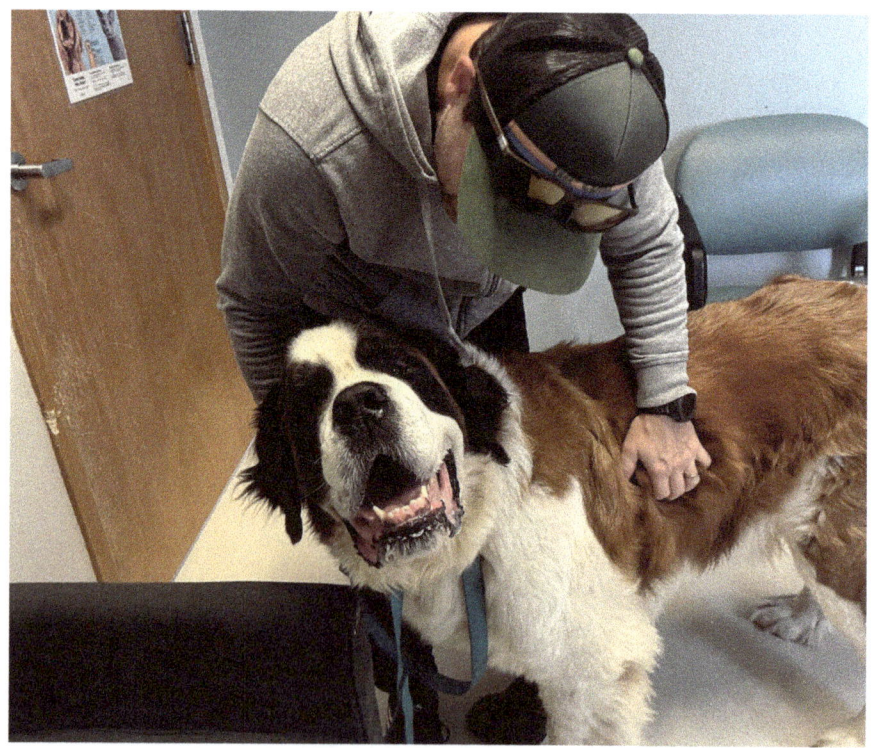

*Opie smiles lovingly after reuniting with Brian following numerous health tests.*

Because of Opie's age and his deep love for swimming, surgery wasn't a viable option. Even if the procedure had been successful, he would no longer have been able to swim due to the high risk of aspiration pneumonia. Brian and I both believed that a life filled with joy, comfort, and love was far more meaningful than an existence that was merely prolonged. We chose to limit his activity and surround him with love.

The next day, we planned to leave Opie behind during our walk, but his heartbreaking howls made us turn back and bring him along. Brian used the tractor to plow trails in the snow, making it easier for Opie to walk with us. As soon as the paths were ready, Opie took off after the tractor alongside the other dogs. When I called out for him to stop, he turned and gave me a look that said, *Why? This is the best fun ever!*

*Left: Opie giving me an inquisitive look, wondering why he had to stay back. Right: Opie (in the back) enjoying life to the fullest running the freshly groomed trails with the rest of his pack.*

Whenever I talked with my dad, he'd always ask how Opie was doing. I'd reply, "Dad, it's unbelievable! He's so happy—like he's been born again!"

I truly believe Opie caught a glimpse of the other side, and that Wilbur gently nudged him back to me.

When Opie turned nine in February, it felt like an even bigger reason to celebrate. I made him his favorite banana birthday cake and bought new beds for Gus, Arthur, Linus, and of course, Opie.

For months before Opie's collapse, we had tried to get him to ride on the back of the tractor because our property is very hilly, and the steep slopes were really challenging for him. But he was always too afraid to try. After his medical incident, though, he realized the rides actually helped him and were for his own good. From that day forward, he would happily walk the flat trails with us but ride the tractor back up the hills, grinning from ear to ear.

*Left: Opie happily accepting a ride on the tractor. Right: Gus, Linus, and Arthur following closely behind, eagerly waiting their turn.*

The other dogs had also been hesitant about riding the tractor, but once they saw Opie enjoying it, they eagerly awaited their turn. Brian and I spent many evenings making sure each dog took his turn as he enjoyed his joyride around the property.

In May of 2025, we were having a wonderful time vacationing in Florida when my mother-in-law phoned us with concerning news. Opie was missing. Opie was never one to wander away, and when Brian's mom informed us that he hadn't shown up at home for dinner, we immediately knew that something was terribly wrong. Without hesitation, Brian and Braydon booked flights home—the thought of Opie alone in the woods was unbearable.

None of us got any sleep. The next day, as Brian and Braydon turned onto our familiar gravel road, their stomachs sank at the sight before them. When we left, everything was just beginning to blossom in early spring, but in only ten days, it had grown wild and unruly. They knew the work ahead would be daunting.

Brian and Braydon spent the entire day combing our property and the surrounding area—searching creeks, ponds, and everything in between. I strongly suspected that Opie might be on the ridge bordering our land, where he had always enjoyed hunting for mushrooms alongside me. Given his age and physical limitations, we felt certain that he was close by. He simply couldn't travel long distances on foot; that was why he always rode on the tractor over challenging terrain.

By the time that daylight faded into night, desperation and defeat over their exhausting yet futile search for Opie plagued Brian and Braydon. They had trekked more than 40,000 steps and covered twenty miles through thick, overgrown woods, high humidity, and swarms of insects. They left every ounce of strength, energy, and determination they had in those now dark and foreboding woods.

The next day we hired Reaves Recovery and Rescue, which is a thermal drone service, to perform an aerial search of our property and the surrounding land. Because there was nothing more that Brian could do on our Indiana property in the search for Opie, he had flown back to rejoin us in Florida while Braydon returned to his job. The drone service connected with us on FaceTime at our condominium so that we could view the aerial search for our missing Saint Bernard in real time. Sadly, they came up empty-handed.

We had known that our chances of finding Opie alive were slim. Opie's love for his pack was immense, and if at all possible, he would have returned home. Our condo lease was expiring, and our vacation was winding down to its admittedly sobering end. It was time to head home.

The twelve-hour drive back to our home was somber and anxious. All that we wanted was to return to our property to resume our grim search. Carly was heartbroken that she was unable to accompany us home, but she was obligated to head directly to a BMX National in Nashville, Tennessee. It was part and parcel of the sacrifice that often comes with being a professional athlete. However, we knew in our hearts, that Carly wouldn't want to miss returning to the same National where Opie had once waited for her at the finish line—and that he wouldn't have wanted her to miss it either.

As we pulled into our driveway, we held our breath. The drone service had suggested that Opie's body might be submerged in our pond, and that at some point his remains could resurface. Thankfully, however, that was not the case.

Our dogs were normally overjoyed to see us after we returned from a trip, but upon our arrival this time their affect was low and somber. Gus seemed almost frantic, with eyes that seemed to plead with us to find Opie. Realizing that our fridge would be empty, my mother-in-law had surprised us with a homemade breakfast casserole to fuel us before we headed out. Shortly after finishing our tasty meal, Brian, Heidi, and I set out on foot, determined to discover the fate of our beloved friend.

I wore my necklace holding Wilbur's ashes and asked him to help bring Opie home.

We left Gus, Arthur, and Linus at home early on in our search. We were well aware that we likely had a long day ahead of us, and we felt that the distance that we would hike in the heat and humidity would be too much for our younger pups. We began by carefully raking every inch of the pond from our pedal boat, with negative results. Brian and I then downloaded an application to our phones that enabled us to track our steps, ensuring that we covered every inch of our property. As we searched, we occasionally encountered tiny, spotted fawns in the foliage—a beautiful sight in the midst of heartbreaking circumstances.

As night fell, our anxiety grew. Heidi was alarmed to discover that multiple ticks were clinging to her, so she left the search to go home and shower. In a last-ditch effort, I suggested to Brian that we bring Gus, Arthur, and Linus along and follow their lead across the property, hoping they might lead us to Opie. Within minutes, the three of them guided us to his body—lying on the ridge where I had first suspected we might find him. Judging by the position of his body, Opie had clearly been on his way home.

Brian sobbed, devastated that he and Braydon had unknowingly walked past Opie's body at least three times during their grim search. Even the thermal drone service we hired had flown their drone directly over the spot—but by then, Opie's body had cooled too much for the heat sensors to detect him. We had envisioned being able to hold our boy one last time, stroking his soft fur and saying goodbye. Sadly, significant decomposition had already taken its ghastly toll. I am grateful that Heidi wasn't with us when we found him; the sight of Opie in that condition would have been far too much for her.

Brian was grief-stricken, shedding tears almost uncontrollably. The dogs gathered around Opie, gently sniffing his body; Linus even gave his ear a soft lick. Although it was heartbreaking, our dogs had found some closure. Gus actually seemed relieved that Opie had finally been located. I remained with the dogs while Brian fetched the tractor, a blanket, and a shovel. While he was gone, I looked online and found a twenty-four-hour pet crematory in Cincinnati and called to let them know we'd be there soon.

Loading Opie's 180-pound body onto the tractor wasn't easy—especially in the condition that he was in—but together, we managed it. I focused on staying strong because we had a job to do. Once Opie was secured on the back of the tractor, I rode with him one last time as the dogs followed closely behind. As difficult as the moment was, all I could see in my mind was the vision of Opie smiling at me, just like he always had when riding on the tractor.

When we returned with Opie's body, Heidi asked if she could see him. I softly told her that she'd be happier remembering him as the big, beautiful boy he had always been. Brian and I moved swiftly to secure his body in the back of the "big red truck," as vultures circled ominously overhead. It was not the outcome we had hoped for over the past several anxiety-ridden days, yet I felt a deep sense of relief that there was closure. After leaving the crematorium, I contacted Carly, my voice trembling as all the pain and heartache came pouring out while I told her everything that had transpired.

It seemed almost unbelievable that we had lost both Wilbur and Opie within just ten months. We were faced with having to accept the fact that our original trio who had endured living in the trailer with us—Wilbur, Opie, and Huckleberry, were now gone. A chapter of our lives had closed. Gus, Arthur, and Linus had some big shoes to fill.

Both losses were tragic, but with Wilbur, we had, in a sense, "played God." By contrast, I found comfort in the knowledge that Opie's time had truly come, and that when it had arrived Opie was out on an adventure, doing what he loved most. The only time that Opie had ever run off before was upon hearing the cry of a fawn. Their screams are similar to that of a small child. After having spotted so many of the baby animals during our search for Opie, it seemed plausible to us that the cry of one of them had triggered his running away to investigate.

We believe that Opie suffered another collapse, similar to the one he had experienced on my birthday, but that this time, Wilbur had given him permission to go. I still find comfort in knowing that, while we could have lost Opie back in January, we were, through some miracle, granted nearly five more months with him; bonus months, so to speak, filled with more love and joyful memories than many dogs experience in a lifetime.

Shortly after Opie had passed, I dreamed that he came right up to my face—his big droopy jowls and wet nose just inches away, with his expression one of pure happiness. I woke up smiling, knowing in my heart that he was okay.

Gus seemed to take Opie's death particularly hard. To him, it must have felt like he had lost his parents. Wilbur and Opie had been by his side since the day he arrived at our home. He had started out as the baby of the pack, but now circumstances had thrust him into the role of being its leader. He seemed confused and a bit uneasy in his new position.

We gave him plenty of extra love, encouragement, and support, especially as he worked through food aggression issues that had never appeared before but surfaced during his transition to pack leader. Together, we made it through the adjustment period, and today, Gus seems to have settled comfortably into his new role as alpha.

He's taken to barking at Arthur and Linus when they get too rowdy and rambunctious, just as Wilbur and Opie used to do with him. Today, watching the three of them interact and grow together is a constant joy. Since Opie's passing, Gus has definitely become more clingy—but we don't mind one bit. We just end up changing our clothes a lot more often. (Kidding… mostly.)

Gus, Arthur, and Linus love roaming our land. With the arrival of late spring and its flow into summer, sweet and succulent wild black raspberries spring up around our property. Every Saint that we've had has a special talent for finding these delectable, sun-warmed treasures and harbors a love for their delicious flavor as they gently nibble at the ripest of the ripe.

*Top left: Wilbur shows Arthur how to find the best raspberries. Top right: Arthur quickly catches on, learning from Wilbur's example. Bottom left: Opie searches for the perfect berry while Arthur enjoys one. Bottom right: Opie and Gus team up to find raspberries together.*

Weekly trips to the nearby Whitewater River with our Saints have become a family tradition. It's the perfect way to keep the dogs' tails wagging and their spirits high. It's incredible to feel their strong, powerful bodies beside us as they skillfully cut through the water. I imagine it must be something like swimming with bears—minus, of course, the fear of being eaten!

*Top: Me, Gus, Linus, and Arthur cooling off with a swim on a hot day. Bottom left: Gus being a total ham, showing off a pair of sunglasses left behind on the riverbank. Bottom right: Linus looking irresistibly cute in his ball cap, keeping his sweet white face safe from the sun.*

Brian and I laugh whenever we think about how we went from cruising around in a sleek Porsche to chugging along in the rust-covered "big red truck" with three Saint Bernards squeezed between us, fur and drool everywhere. It is quite the spectacle, and we wouldn't trade it for anything! Every time we pull up to a stoplight or into a gas station, people's jaws drop in disbelief with many rubbing their eyes like they can't believe what they're seeing. Brian and I shoot each other a look, raise our eyebrows, and give them a friendly wave—it never gets old.

*Top: Gus, Linus, Brian, and me in the "big red truck". Bottom left: Linus resting his head on Brian's shoulder, eager to see where today's adventure takes us. Bottom right: Gus, Arthur, and Linus piling into the "big red truck".*

*Gus looks for encouragement from Brian as he swims across the Whitewater River.*

Currently we're searching for a transit van to make getting around a little easier—and I'm already plotting to convince Brian to paint "The Saint Bernard Mobile" on the side. Who am I kidding? He doesn't stand a chance—I'm definitely going to make it happen! I truly believe that if you can picture it in your mind, you can breathe it into existence. Everything starts with a vision—and when you chase that vision with relentless passion and unwavering drive, there's very little that you can't achieve.

Gus, Arthur, and Linus all wear GPS tracking collars now—just in case. Losing Opie reminded us how quickly things can change, and how powerless you can feel in those moments. Some things are beyond value—peace of mind is one of them.

Raising Saint Bernards has truly been a gift, and I'm so thankful that I never gave up on my core childhood dream. My life would feel far less complete without them. I used to fear that after losing Wilbur, I might never be able to love another dog as deeply, but that love has only continued to grow.

Each Saint is uniquely special, but the qualities Wilbur instilled in them continue to shine brightly. It's truly heartwarming to see the essence of my dear Wilbur reflected in each of them. Although Linus never had the chance to learn directly from Wilbur, the lessons reach him through his elder pack members.

*Left: The original trio—Huckleberry, Wilbur, and Opie (left to right). Right: Today's trio—Gus, Linus, and Arthur (left to right), carrying on the legacy.*

My Saints have taught me so much about resilience, gratitude, and joy. I love life and genuinely wake up happy and excited every single day! If you don't feel that way, it's time to make a change—find what truly fuels your soul and lights that fire inside of you. Refuse to settle when it comes to your dreams or becoming the best version of yourself. We have more control over our destinies than we realize—when we choose consciously and keep a positive spirit, everything falls into place. Happiness looks different for everyone, and you deserve to discover your own.

Brian and I placed a cross in the woods where we found Opie. It's become a special place for us—we walk there often, and sometimes we leave him a banana. It still makes me sad to see that so much of his fur remains, but knowing the kind soul that he was, I think he'd be glad that little animals are using it to build nests to keep their babies warm.

*Arthur, Gus, and Linus visiting the special spot where we found our sweet Opie.*

One morning, during one of my walks to his spot—where I often find myself praying—a thought hit me out of nowhere, as if dropped straight into my heart: *I'm going to write a book called* **The Saint Bernard Memoirs**. When I got home and told Brian, he didn't hesitate. "Do it," he said. And just like that, he handed me his laptop.

### Fernando

Our cat, Fernando, deserves a chapter of his own. The name Fernando means "brave traveler" or "daring explorer," and it suits him perfectly.

In 2013, just a month after we brought Wilbur home, Brian discovered that mice had taken up residence in the engine of his Porsche, causing significant damage. Neither of us had ever been cat people—we're both severely allergic—but desperate times call for desperate measures. So, we headed to a local animal shelter and adopted a long-haired black cat, hoping he'd solve our mouse problem.

When we mentioned our plan to the woman working at the shelter, she replied in a voice dripping with condescension, "You know, not all cats chase mice." Well—let me tell you something, honey—Fernando chased anything with legs within a five-mile radius. We paid five dollars for him, and it was the best five dollars we'd ever spent. He was on a mission from day one.

*Wilbur and Fernando fast became friends. Fernando quickly became Wilbur's shadow.*

Before we left the shelter, they told us they'd follow up in forty-eight hours to check on how Fernando was settling in. Having no real clue as to how cats operate, I had naively assumed that if I put food out, he'd just hang around our home. Wrong. He disappeared almost immediately, and I spent the next two days anxiously watching the clock.

As the forty-eight-hour mark approached, I started to panic. The shelter would be calling any minute. Then, just ten minutes before the phone rang, Fernando casually reappeared like nothing had happened. I picked up the call and calmly said, "Everything is going wonderfully," hoping they couldn't hear the relief in my voice.

At first, we wondered if we'd made a mistake. Fernando was making sinister, feral sounds at Wilbur through his crate. It seemed like the two would never get along. But within a month, everything changed—they were playing together and napping side by side in the sun, like a pair of old and trusted friends.

A couple of years after we adopted Fernando, he was struck by a car. Upon impact, his hip popped out of its socket. The vet was able to put it back in, but when it slipped out again, surgery became necessary. Fernando had to wear a cone, but that didn't stop him from pulling out all of his stitches.

We took him back to the vet, and this time they used staples. Heidi even taped a school folder around the cone he had to wear to keep him from ripping the staples out. Somehow, however, Fernando was resourceful enough to find a way to do just that. With no other options left, Brian and I ended up supergluing his skin together— and, surprisingly, it actually worked!

Fernando loved Wilbur, and followed us through the neighborhood on our walks. When we moved from our home into the single-wide, Brian sold his Porsche. (We always joke that we traded Brian's Porsche for a trailer.) Fernando had earned his keep. He did his job, and we loved him for it. When it came time to move, we hoped he'd want to stick around. We knew he'd love the wide-open spaces, full of rodents to chase. An added bonus would be his being far safer from the dangers of heavy traffic. We remembered our dismay when he first disappeared for forty-eight hours after we brought him home. We had learned our lesson, and we were smarter this time. We armed ourselves with allergy pills, and, determined not to risk losing him again, we kept him inside the trailer with us for three full weeks.

Fernando was always incredibly patient with the Saint Bernard puppies we brought home. No matter how much they pounced upon, chewed on, or chased him, he took it in stride—only giving them a well-deserved swat when he'd finally had enough. He seemed to understand they were just babies. Each night, he'd take turns curling up with one of them, sharing his warmth and his companionship. I have so many photos of him sandwiched between Wilbur and Opie, fast asleep, like he belonged there—and he did.

*Left: Gus receives a well-deserved swat. Right: Fernando looks at Arthur, unamused.*

He came with us on every walk, keeping pace as if he were just another member of the pack. It was always a sight: this sleek black cat walking confidently alongside a group of giant Saint Bernards. More often than not, he had a signature blob of drool on his head—but that's part of loving a Saint Bernard. And love them he did, fully and fiercely.

*Left: Huckleberry and Fernando. Right: Opie and Fernando walking together.*

When one of the dogs was hurt or feeling unwell, Fernando always seemed to know. He would quietly find them, curl up by their side, and gently lick their paws or ears, offering whatever comfort he could. It was such a quiet, pure kind of love—the kind that never asked for attention; he simply gave what was needed.

*Left: Fernando snuggled up next to Huckleberry after his surgery. Right: Fernando checking in on Wilbur after an emergency bloat procedure.*

*Opie and Fernando*

When it came to tormenting Fernando, Linus was the most relentless. He rarely passed up an opportunity to pester Fernando, pushing his tolerance to its limits. On the night that we found Opie's body, however, something profoundly changed. That night, Fernando chose to sleep inside of Linus's crate with him. I attempted to remove him before the dogs' bedtime, but Fernando made it clear to me that he was staying. Somehow he knew that Linus needed him.

*Left: Fernando gives Wilbur a lick. Right: Linus sneaks in a quick lick to Fernando.*

Fernando is thirteen now, and he's the last living thread connecting us to those days in the trailer. He's been with us through every chapter, witnessed our every joy and heartache, and through it all, he's steadfastly loved each and every one of us. He's not just our cat—he's our constant, and the heart of a multitude of treasured memories.

## Acknowledgments

I'm incredibly grateful to all of you who took the time to read my book and join me on this adventure.

Above all, I want to thank God. I prayed daily for His guidance and for the Holy Spirit to dwell within me and direct my hand as I wrote. I continue to thank Him every day for the trailer that served its purpose and helped us build our dream home.

A special thank you to my husband, Brian, whose constant support inspires me to pursue my dreams without hesitation. He has given me the freedom to do so.

To my daughters, Carly and Heidi—my best friends and two of the most amazing humans I know—you are a daily reminder that I got something right.

Thank you to my dad, Mike Glaser, a brilliant writer in his own right, who guided me through every edit. I hope I've inherited even a fraction of his talent.

To my mom, Connie Glaser—thank you for being the very first person to read my book and for offering such thoughtful, encouraging feedback. As a stay-at-home mom, you showed me the true value of being present for your family, and you're the reason I've always understood how important that role is.

To my mother-in-law, Vicki Kane, thank you for capturing our holiday memories through your photography and for looking after our dogs so we can continue to chase our dreams.

A heartfelt thank you to my father-in-law, Mike Kane, who would drop everything at a moment's notice to help Brian with any project we had. Your selflessness and support have meant the world to us.

To my brother, Johnny Glaser—thank you for the countless hours you spent helping Brian frame our house. Your time, hard work, and dedication will always be part of the foundation of our home, both literally and figuratively.

I'm also grateful to Braydon Hayes and Eli Aston for bringing so much happiness into our daughters' lives.

Thank you to the incredibly talented Sarah Brantley for painting Jenny's Dream, the artwork featured on my cover. The painting includes Wilbur and Huckleberry, and when Sarah first asked to create it—based on a photo I'd posted on Facebook—she had no idea they were my two dogs who had passed away. Seeing the finished piece felt like a visit from them.

Thank you to Rhonda Hensley for finding our sweet puppy, Opie, and for being an endless source of wisdom. Our animals bring wonderful people into our lives, and Rhonda is one of those treasures.

A sincere thank you to Jackie Knopp for years of commenting, "You need to write a book!" on my Facebook posts. Thank you for being that constant whisper in the back of my mind.

A heartfelt thank you to all the breeders who entrusted our family with the beautiful lives you helped create: Shawn Pellerin, Jennifer Hanger, Christyna Laws, Brittany Bertothy, Nathalie and Dana Wilson, and Melanie Stavert.

Last, but certainly not least, thank you to my dogs—Wilbur, Opie, Huckleberry, Gus, Arthur, and Linus. You are the heart and soul of this book, filling my life with joy and making me a better person each day.

For more Saint Bernard adventures, feel free to follow my Facebook page, Jenny Kane– Author. We're currently working on an exciting new project called The Green Bernard—a grass tennis court with its own Facebook page as well. If you have any questions, don't hesitate to reach out to me at jenny@thegreenbernard.com

# In Remembrance of Wilbur "Willy Woo"

April 10, 2013 – July 6, 2024

## The Last Battle

If it should be that I grow weak,
And pain should keep me from my sleep,
Then you must do what must be done,
For this last battle cannot be won.
You will be sad, I understand;
Don't let your grief then stay your hand.
For this day more than all the rest,
Your love for me must stand the test.
We've had so many happy years -
What is to come can hold no fears.
You'd not want me to suffer so;
The time has come, so let me go.
Take me where my needs they'll tend
And please stay with me until the end.
Hold me firm and speak to me
Until my eyes no longer see.
I know in time that you will see
The kindness that you did for me.
Although my tail its last has waved,
From pain and suffering I've been saved.
Please do not grieve - it must be you
Who had this painful thing to do.
We've been so close, we two, these years -
Don't let your heart hold back its tears.

*Author — unknown*

# In Remembrance of Opie "Oper Doos"

February 12, 2016 – May 18, 2025

I stood by your bed last night, I came to have a peep.
I could see that you were crying...you found it hard to sleep.
I whined to you softly as you brushed away a tear.
"It's me, I haven't left you...I'm well, I'm fine, I'm here."
I was close to you at breakfast, I watched you pour the tea.
You were thinking of the many times, your hands reached down to me.
I was with you at the shops today, your arms were getting sore.
I longed to take your parcels, I wish I could do more.
I was with you at my grave today, you tend it with such care.
I want to reassure you that I am not lying there.
I walked with you toward the house, as you fumbled for your key,
I gently put my paw on you. I smiled and said, "It's me."
You looked so very tired, and sank into a chair.
I tried so hard to let you know that I was standing there.
It's possible for me to be so near you every day.
To say to you with certainty, "I never went away."
You sat there very quietly, then smiled, I think you knew...
In the stillness of that evening, I was very close to you.
The day is over... I smile and watch you yawning
And say, "Goodnight, God bless, I'll see you in the morning."
And when the time is right for you to cross the brief divide,
I'll rush across to greet you and we will stand, side-by-side.
I have so many things to show you, there is so much for you to see.
Be patient, live your journey out... then come home to be with me.

*Author — unknown*

## In Remembrance of Huckleberry "Huckles"

March 18, 2019 – November 24, 2021

Moon river, wider than a mile
I'm crossing you in style some day
Oh, dream maker, you heart breaker
Wherever you're goin', I'm goin' your way
Two drifters, off to see the world
There's such a lot of world to see
We're after the same rainbow's end
Waitin' 'round the bend
My huckleberry friend
Moon river and me

*(Lyrics taken from the famous song "Moon River" written by Johnny Mercer with music by Henry Mancini)*

*2017: The year our matching Christmas pajama photos began!*

*2018: Priscilla the chinchilla posing on Heidi's head.*

*2019: Huckleberry joined our family.*

*It became a tradition for Brian's parents to join in on our Christmas shenanigans—snapping our family photo and then sharing lattes and Saint Bernard pancakes together.*

*2020: Fernando the cat partook in the fun.*

*2021: Braydon and Carly started dating. We took our photo early this year due to Huckleberry's declining health. We lost him a few days later.*

*2022: Eli and Heidi started dating and he became familiar with our family traditions. Gus joined our family.*

*2023: The definition of love.*

*2024: A bittersweet year. We lost our sweet Wilbur. Arthur and Linus joined our family.*

# Wilbur's Favorite Pumpkin Dog Cake

## Ingredients

Cake

- ¼ cup melted coconut oil (cooled)
- 1 cup unsweetened almond milk
- ½ cup plain pumpkin purée
- ½ cup pure maple syrup
- 1 teaspoon apple cider vinegar
- 1½ cups all-purpose flour
- 1 teaspoon baking soda
- ½ teaspoon baking powder
- ½ teaspoon ground cinnamon
- ¼ teaspoon salt

Frosting

- ⅔ cup Greek yogurt
- 1 tablespoon maple syrup

## Directions

1. Preheat the oven to 350°F. Lightly grease three 4-inch pans or one 8-inch pan, then line with parchment.
2. In a large mixing bowl, whisk the almond milk, pumpkin, maple syrup, and vinegar. Stir in the cooled coconut oil.
3. In a separate bowl, combine the flour, baking soda, baking powder, cinnamon, and salt.
4. Add the dry mixture to the wet ingredients, stirring gently until just combined—small lumps are fine.
5. Divide the batter between your prepared pans and tap the pans lightly to smooth the surface.
6. Bake:
   - 4-inch pans: 27–32 minutes
   - 8-inch pan: about 40 minutes

   The cake is done when a toothpick inserted in the center comes out clean.

7. Allow the cakes to cool for 10 minutes in the pan, then transfer to a rack to cool fully.
8. For the frosting, mix the Greek yogurt and maple syrup until smooth.
9. Once cooled, level the cakes if desired, then frost and stack.

*From: TheAlmondeater.com*

# Opie's Favorite Banana Dog Cake

## Ingredients
- 2 very ripe bananas
- ⅓ cup melted coconut oil
- ½ cup water
- 1½ cups unbleached flour
- 1 teaspoon baking soda
- 1 tablespoon apple cider vinegar

## Directions
1. Preheat the oven to 350°F. Grease an 8×8-inch or 9×9-inch pan.
2. Mash the bananas until smooth. Mix in the melted oil and water.
3. Add flour and baking soda; stir just to combine.
4. Stir in the vinegar and immediately pour the batter into your prepared pan.
5. Bake for 25–30 minutes, or until a toothpick inserted in the center comes out clean.
6. Cool in the pan, then transfer to a rack to cool completely.

*From: VeganDollhouse.com*

# Huckleberry's Favorite Carrot Peanut Butter Dog Cake

## Ingredients
- 1 large egg
- ¼ cup natural peanut butter (xylitol-free)
- ¼ cup canola oil
- ⅓ cup honey
- 1 cup shredded carrots
- 1 cup whole wheat flour
- 1 teaspoon baking soda

## Directions
1. Preheat the oven to 350°F. Lightly grease a 6-inch round pan.
2. In a medium bowl, whisk the egg, peanut butter, oil, and honey until smooth.
3. Stir in the shredded carrots.
4. Add the flour and baking soda, mixing just until incorporated.
5. Spread the batter into the pan and bake for 40 minutes, or until a toothpick comes out clean.
6. Cool 5–10 minutes in the pan, then move to a rack to finish cooling.

# Gus's Favorite Sweet Potato Apple Dog Cake

## Ingredients

Dry
- 1 cup oat flour
- ¾ teaspoon baking soda

Wet
- 1 egg
- ½ cup unsweetened applesauce
- ½ cup sweet potato purée
- ¼ cup peanut butter (xylitol-free)
- ⅛ cup coconut oil

Frosting
- ½ cup unsweetened Greek yogurt
- ¼ cup peanut butter (xylitol-free)

## Directions
1. Preheat oven to 350°F. Grease two 6-inch round pans.
2. In a small bowl, whisk together the oat flour and baking soda.
3. In a larger bowl, combine the egg, applesauce, sweet potato, peanut butter, and coconut oil.
4. Add the dry mix to the wet ingredients in small portions, stirring between additions.
5. Divide the batter evenly between the pans.
6. Bake for 18–22 minutes, or until a toothpick comes out clean.
7. Cool in the pans for 10 minutes; then transfer to a rack to cool completely.
8. Stir together the yogurt and peanut butter to make the frosting, then refrigerate until use.

## To Assemble
- Level the tops if needed.
- Spread frosting between the layers and over the outside of the cake.

# Arthur's Favorite Blueberry Dog Cake with Maple Frosting

## Ingredients

Cake
- 1 cup all-purpose flour
- 1 teaspoon baking soda
- ½ teaspoon baking powder
- ½ teaspoon ground cinnamon
- ⅛ teaspoon salt
- ½ cup unsweetened applesauce
- ⅓ cup honey
- ¼ cup vegetable oil
- 1 large egg (room temperature)
- ½ teaspoon alcohol-free vanilla (optional)
- 1½ cups fresh blueberries, divided

Frosting
- 8 oz reduced-fat cream cheese, softened
- 2–3 tablespoons maple syrup

## Directions
1. Preheat the oven to 350°F. Grease and flour two 6-inch round pans.
2. Whisk together flour, baking soda, baking powder, cinnamon, and salt.
3. In another bowl, beat the applesauce, honey, oil, egg, and vanilla until smooth.
4. Add the dry mix gradually, stirring between additions.
5. Fold in 1 cup of the blueberries.
6. Divide the batter between the pans and bake 22–28 minutes, or until a toothpick comes out clean.
7. Cool in the pans for 10 minutes, then transfer to a rack.
8. For the frosting, beat the cream cheese with 2 tablespoons maple syrup, adding a bit more for sweetness or softness as needed.

## To Assemble
- Frost the tops of both layers, stack, and garnish with the remaining blueberries.

*From: UrbanBakes.com*

# Linus's Favorite Strawberry & Cream Pupcake

## Ingredients

Cake
- 12 medium strawberries, divided
- ¼ cup softened coconut oil
- 2 tablespoons honey
- 1 egg
- ½ cup almond milk
- 1 cup whole wheat flour
- 1 teaspoon baking powder

Frosting
- ¾ cup Greek yogurt
- Half of the strawberry purée
- ¼ cup xylitol-free peanut butter
- Small dog biscuits (optional, for decorating)

## Directions

1. Preheat the oven to 350°F. Grease a 6-inch round pan.
2. Remove strawberry stems and pulse in a blender until finely chopped. Divide the purée equally—half for the batter, half for the frosting.
3. Cream together the coconut oil and honey. Mix in the egg and almond milk.
4. Add the flour and baking powder, stirring until just combined.
5. Fold in half of the strawberry purée.
6. Pour into the pan and bake 25–30 minutes, or until the cake is set and a toothpick comes out clean.
7. Cool completely before frosting.
8. Mix the remaining strawberry purée with the Greek yogurt and spread over the top.
9. Coat the sides of the cake in a thin layer of peanut butter and press small biscuits around the outside if desired.

*From: SprinklesandSeasalt.com*

www.ingramcontent.com/pod-product-compliance
Lightning Source LLC
Chambersburg PA
CBHW051636120626
46551CB00014B/2103